RECOVERY

*Understanding and Dealing
With Life's Traumas*

RECOVERY

*Understanding and Dealing
with Life's Traumas*

Clifford E. Turner, Ph.D.

The Wine Press
Whitehouse Station, New Jersey

RECOVERY
*Understanding and Dealing
with Life's Traumas*

Copyright © 2000 by Clifford E. Turner, Ph.D.

Published by The Wine Press, an imprint of End Time Wave Publications, P.O. Box 848, Whitehouse Station, N.J. 08889.

ISBN 1-889389-19-6

Printed in the United States of America

Unless otherwise indicated, Bible quotations are taken from The Thompson Chain-Reference Bible, copyright © 1908, 1917, 1929, 1934, 1957, 1964, 1982, and 1988 by the B.B. Kirkbride Bible Company, Inc., and are used by permission.

Third Printing 2001

Dedication

I dedicate this book to my wife, Darlyn, my best friend. I will always be thankful to God for joining us together. Thank you for your prayers and ministry to me and our children. You are truly a "virtuous woman."

To our nine children: Deleia, Christy, Denise, Victoria, Clifford, Jr., Danaya, Jonathan, Darry, and Jenny. Daddy loves each of you and appreciates your sacrifice as your Mom and I fulfill the call of God on our lives.

A special thanks to Pastor Sheraine Lathon for her diligence, hard work, and persistence, without which this book could never have been published; to Evangelist Marcia Etherly, and Pastor Perry Mallory who also aided in the publishing of this work; to Evangelist Carole Harrell and the Editing Ministry; to Mother Gertrude L. Price for her encouragement; and to the entire Liberty Temple Full Gospel Church "Recovery Class" and staff.

Above all, I thank God, our Father; our Lord Jesus Christ for His saving grace; and the Holy Spirit for His faithfulness in comforting me as I underwent my RECOVERY!

TABLE OF CONTENTS

Preface

In life, we learn to deal with social skills and normal, everyday emotional ups and downs -- emotions we experience and those we see in others. Job said, "Man that is born of woman is of few days and full of trouble" (Job 14:1). So, that "full" of trouble we experience will not be normal or everyday -- it will be devastating, traumatic, alarming, shocking, and horrifying, to say the least.

We learn to handle everyday problems; sometimes we learn the hard way – from experience. But what about the "big boys," major traumas and losses in life? Most of us are not prepared to deal with life's tragedies. We know what to do for a cold, how to handle a disagreement, where to get help for a toothache. But, what do we do when we experience such trauma that our spirit, soul, and body are thrown out of whack? How do we recover from devastation in life?

Paul said:

"Blessed be God, even the Father of our Lord Jesus Christ, the Father of mercies, and the God of all comfort; Who comforteth us in all our tribulation, that we may be able to comfort them which are in any trouble by the comfort wherewith we ourselves are comforted of God. For as the sufferings of Christ abound in us, so our consolation also aboundeth by Christ. And whether we be afflicted it is for your consolation and salvation, which is effectual in the enduring of the same sufferings which we also suffer: or whether we be comforted, it is for your consolation and salvation."

(II Corinthians 1:3-6)

In RECOVERY, I am sharing with you what the Holy Spirit shared with me as I recovered from the greatest loss in my life -- the death of my wife, my best friend of twenty years. The main area in which God ministered to me was in the area of my emotions. My emotions were shattered. Without my emotions being whole, everything and everybody in my life was affected. But, thanks be to God, He healed me. And in receiving my healing, my misery has become my ministry. I can now give to you what I received from God through years of tears and struggles.

My hope is for my readers to go on with God, no matter what you've been through; and to be some of the most anointed people in the world to deal with inner conflicts brought on by a season of hurt, whether it's in your life or, as ministers of reconciliation, in the lives of others.

This book is written as a training manual to train up God's people to minister effectively to the hurting and wounded. You will find questions following every several chapters and the answer key in the appendix.

Therefore, I promise you, brother and sister, that with the help of God, you are going to be awesomely used by God, because this book is enough spiritual dynamite to blow the devil to Kingdom come! As you listen, hear, and understand how to recover, the Holy Spirit will show you faces of people who need this kind of ministering. But don't you know the first person He will show you is YOU! That's because the Word of God is a mirror. The thing you don't like in another person is a reflection of what you don't like in yourself. The area you recognize that another person needs inner healing is usually the area in which you need it yourself. That's okay. We all need recovery. So, let's move on, gain the understanding we need, and let the healing begin!

Human Emotions and the Soul

Introduction

There are so many facets of the human emotion that we witness daily without understanding the significance of what we see. The human emotion is an area where most of us are uninformed and uneducated, because we have not been taught about our emotions. Most of the time, we do not know how to accept and deal with people who have emotional problems. Turbulent events have transpired in our lives that have caused emotional scars. Confrontation, rejection, disappointment, deception, and many other forms of personal denial have left us in a position where we have serious problems relating to others.

In order to seriously lead us onto the road of recovery, I will lay a foundation of truth that will include some pertinent facts concerning human emotions and the structure of the soul. The shadows of skepticism and uncertainty that we have allowed to exist concerning ourselves have to be pulled into the "light of day" -- into the light of order and balance.

I am all for being spiritual, because I know that God has made us spiritual beings and will, therefore, include some spiritual matters as we progress into this teaching. Yet, as saints of God, we have often over-spiritualized events that are only natural occurrences. What we need to avoid is becoming overly "supernatural." God has made us natural beings, as well as spiritual beings. The Bible says "first the natural, then the spiritual" (I Corinthians 15:46). If we lose sight of the earthly side of our being, the natural man will not receive the appropriate care he or she needs. God wants us to know that we should not deal with things that are spiritual, naturally; neither should we deal with natural things, spiritually.

Proper nurture of the soul begins with an honest appraisal

of our natural emotions. And, as we progress, it will be important to remember that all references to the mind also include the soul. Regardless of how guilty some Word of Faith teachings have made us feel about our natural emotions, the truth is that we are human, and most of God's people are hurting somewhere in their souls. Some of us are afflicted and limited in how far we can progress in God because of sensitive and painful wounds from the past. We've never been healed from them and we don't really understand how significant they have been in hindering us and making it difficult for us to deal with life's experiences. If the people of God do not get some help in the area of the psyche, in the area of the soul, we are headed toward self-destruction. This book is my attempt to get you to pinpoint and locate where you are emotionally so that you can receive your healing and, in turn, go out and reach scores of others.

Chapter One

Loss

Focus on not what was lost,
but focus on what remains!

By definition, a loss is the damage, trouble, disadvantage, and deprivation that is caused by losing something. When you lose something or someone very precious to you, or if something or someone has been taken from you or been denied you, you have suffered a loss. All of us who have held people or things very close to us in love have suffered loss. On one end of the spectrum, we might have experienced the death of a loved one. At the other end of the spectrum, there might have been the loss of an inanimate object. You might think that the loss of a thing could not be as damaging as losing someone important in your life, but if that thing was yours and you loved it and lost it, you experienced a loss.

EMOTIONAL INTENSITY AND LOSS

When we see people afraid, angry, or depressed, it is indicative of loss in their lives. Of course, some of us react stronger because our losses are deeper.

To illustrate what I mean, in a hypothetical situation, suppose I fall and scrape my knee, coming down the stairs, just one step away from a carpeted floor. I get up and start walking and I'm fine. I can deal with that. Now, that same evening, I fall off the floor of a four-story building. Do you expect me to get up and react the same way I did when I fell onto the carpeting? Of course, not. Since it was a deeper trauma, my reaction to it will be more intense. The greater the trauma, the longer it will take to be healed from it. You cannot expect to be healed from a deep emotional trauma the same way that you got healed from one that was not as emotional. But, no one wants to lose, no one wants to suffer loss. So, we react to loss; whether our reaction is slight or intense, we still have an emotional response to the losses in our lives.

Loss is also a type of cataclysmic upheaval. It is like a child playing with blocks. He may have designed a structure with which he was content. But, suddenly, another child may approach him and throw all the blocks in the air and watch them fall in an unpredictable pattern. The first child may experience anger, frustration, and loss, but if he desires to continue his game, he has to begin the tedious process of reconstruction.

God will build on the ashes of devastation!

Chapter Two

Grief

God cannot change your past,
But God can heal your past
if you give it to Him!

According to the Merriam-Webster Dictionary, grief is a deep and poignant distress caused by or as if by bereavement, an unfortunate outcome, disaster, mishap, misadventure, trouble, or annoyance. Our losses cause grief.

Grief is hard work. Grief recovery is so demanding that you will look for any way to get out of it -- any way to keep from going through it. Yet, the way out of grief is always through it.

Effective grief-work is never done alone. You should never, ever attempt to go through any emotional problems by yourself. Have a support group. Submit to clergy or professional therapy. Being saved does not preempt you from getting professional help if it is needed. I believe anyone suffering grief needs to get some help. Some may need one encouraging conversation; others may need extended therapy.

Nobody but you knows the extent to which you are

perplexed, oppressed, or depressed. So, get the help. There are no shortcuts to a healthy and full life after a major loss.

None of us want to face grief. We don't want to feel the loneliness, the headaches, and heartaches it brings. The common tendency in grief is to try to avoid it. We strive to get over and through it quickly. None of us really want to deal with grief, so we try to "wait" it out. You can't "wait" out grief. Time and Jesus heals. Working through grief with the aid of the Holy Spirit can heal the deep wounds, enabling you to recover and get a true sense of balance again.

If you are working through a major loss and feel comfortable, then that's a danger signal. In other words, when you've gone through something traumatic in your life, it takes you time to heal -- you don't have the strength, you don't have the full accessibility of your faculties as you typically would have, and that is normal. But, when you come through a major loss and you say nothing is bothering you, and it's business as usual, you're in trouble, because you're probably in some form of denial. You're probably burying something that will become apparent later. That's like seeing someone get run over by a car and then seeing that same person on the track team the next day. You'd say, "No. Something is wrong here!" You don't expect to have pneumonia in the morning and then back to work on a construction job by noontime. Either you didn't have pneumonia or something is mighty wrong with you! Healing is a process, and it never occurs in a short period of time.

It's natural for all of us to want to hurry up and get through some things, but guess what? You can't hurry love. You can't hurry a healing either. All that is going to happen is that you will rewound yourself and exacerbate the problem.

It's time to check yourself to see if you're trying to skirt around problems. Are you trying to dig a grave for your problems in your subconscious? The truth of the matter is that you can't. Going through the experience is the only lasting way out of grief. This is the healthy response -- "to go through it."

What God doesn't deliver you from, He wants you to go through. And He will take you through, but you have to be vulnerable to get healed. You've got to find someone you can trust and open up to. Don't ever feel that your help can come by distancing and alienating yourself from people. Satan does his best work in isolation, when you have separated yourself from those who care about you. The Bible says, "A brother is raised up for adversity"(Proverbs 17:17). God has raised up somebody to stand with you during that crisis, even if it's nothing more than to give a listening ear. I discovered that never in my life did I feel like talking so much until I had gone through a major crisis. There were some things that were in me that I knew I had to get out of me. If they didn't get out, I know they would have killed me.

Communicating our emotions is not always easy. Men are especially very bad in communicating at the level of our emotions because society tells us that we are supposed to be so macho and strong. Holding our emotions within can attribute to a lot of strokes and heart attacks in men because we are not venting or releasing our anxieties, fears, and angers.

Do not try to avoid grieving, but face it head on. You can get back on top of life again. Your path to recovery will have ups and downs, but if you stay with it, you will emerge stronger than when you started. Allow the months to come and go. If your grief was coupled with sleeplessness, you will start sleeping better again. Lost appetites will eventually return.

Sometimes we encounter grief from the perspective of dealing with a loved one going through the grieving process. You may have married a man or woman who has gone through a traumatic experience and they no longer have a sexual appetite. That part of them has shut down. There are a lot of men who are impotent and don't understand what's happening to their bodies. Brothers, you can also attribute this to a lot of stress in your life. There is a medically defined occurrence in which your body involuntarily starts to transfer energy in the most needed direction. In other words, your body says, "You don't need energy for sex, so I won't release blood in that part of your body."

For example, let's just say that you sit down to eat at a picnic and you are very hungry. All of a sudden, you see a big rattlesnake easing toward you. What does your body do? Your body gives you the necessary strength to get up and move very fast. Now, the moment you are no longer in danger of the snake, you realize that you are not hungry any more. You lose your appetite.

Sisters, your body will do that, too. When your body feels it does not need sex, it won't give you any desire for sex. It won't give you any strength for it. It's like the body takes care of itself in this area. If you try to physically force your body past your emotions, you will just be embarrassed because your emotions and your sex life are tied in together. If you don't articulate to your husband that you are going through something emotionally, he's not going to understand why your body won't respond. He may think that you no longer find him desirable, or he may think that you just don't want to cooperate with him. In any event, he will ultimately feel highly insulted.

When we have gone through hurts, we must articulate what we've gone through to our loved ones (particularly our spouse), so they can help us through it. Never take for granted or assume that they are "supposed" to know. If you have very little desire for sex, let your spouse know. Ideally, tell your prospective spouse about your feelings of impotency before marriage. Neither spouses nor prospective spouses may have the patience to go through your therapy development. How long will your husband have to wait before you come out of your season where you don't want to have sex? How long will your wife have to wait until you're able to perform? Not to tell them is unfair. Not to tell them before marriage is unfair. That's like marrying someone whom has never told you that they have Herpes or AIDS. True, they may not want to go through the changes of being married to you once they know the facts, but give them the opportunity to decide. Keeping such things secret may create a disaster later.

My intentions are not to perplex you with sexual hang-ups, but a lot of God's children have problems in this area. Men definitely don't want to talk about the problems of impotence. I don't care how "powerful" you normally are as a sex partner, when you're tired, your body just won't cooperate with you. I don't care what your eyes want, your body just won't cooperate. It says, "You don't have enough good sense to get some rest, so, I'm going to get some." When you're grieving, you feel tired because grief is very heavy. Tiredness is one of the ways grief manifests itself naturally. Your fatigue, however, won't last forever. To get through grief, you need:

A SUPPORT GROUP, A PASTOR, OR COUNSELING

TO DRINK ADEQUATE AMOUNTS OF WATER
Doctors and psychologists say that when you are grieving, it dehydrates your body. You need to replenish these fluids back into your body. You need to drink 8-10 glasses of water daily.

TO FOLLOW AN ADEQUATE NUTRITIONAL PLAN
Avoid junk foods, fatty foods, sugars, caffeine and alcohol. You can prolong your season of grief by not eating right.

TO GET SUFFICIENT AMOUNTS OF REST
Rest is the foundation of health. Learn how to take breaks; schedule time for rest. Schedule vacations.

There is no point of working hard if you don't reward yourself. Have a reward system. You can't afford not to take vacations. So many times you can punish your body by keeping it in the "up" mode for weeks and months when God only designed it to be "up" for a few hours. Many of you are just "getting by" because you're young, but you will pay for the abuse that you're doing to your body when you get older.

GET ADEQUATE EXERCISE WITHIN THE BOUNDS OF YOUR LIMITATIONS

God's people sometimes don't like to exercise. God's people are often lazy when it comes to exercise. It's an attitude. Your attitude is bad about your own body. Twenty minutes of cardiovascular activity a day will help you. Don't be in bondage about what you can't do. When you exercise, this is the body's way of releasing a lot of stress. You will rest better, too.

LETTING GO

Through the entire healing process, you can grow and change. One of life's most valuable lessons is learning how to let go. I Thessalonians 5:21b says, "Hold fast that which is good." If grief and anger are allowed to persist, they will turn ugly. And that's not good. You will find yourself attacking both the people who you hold responsible for your bad feelings as well as innocent bystanders. There is no magic formula to letting go of anger or learning how to let go. You have to want to give it up. You have to choose being "happy" over being right. Some of us are miserable because we want to be right; we want to prove our point. Sometimes letting go means making a choice: be "happy" or be right.

Some of us are so stubborn and so proud that we would rather be dead than to give in. You can end up "dead" being right. You may say, "But they did me wrong. They did this to me and that." And because of what they did, you're harboring anger and prolonging your grief. God has taught me to pray for the people that provoke me. Learn how to pray. When you pray, the Holy Ghost helps you "get out of flesh." In the natural, you cannot pray for your enemies. It takes the Holy Ghost for you to do that. Learn how to let go of people. God said, "Vengeance is mine" (Romans 12:19). Nobody gets away with anything, especially against a child of God. If we know that, then why don't we just let God have His way in folks' lives? God has a way of whipping people, so stop waiting for people to die! Let it go!

When you don't let go of people, places, and things, you

chain yourself to them. You make yourself a victim of circumstances instead of a person in charge of his or her destiny. In order to get rid of the victimized mentality, you have to learn how to look forward; look ahead. You have to assume the point of view (rightly or wrongly) that you are not a victim. You have control over your own life. You can take charge. You can change your attitude from negative to positive.

Letting go just means that it makes no sense in holding on, because it will only keep you "stuck." So, do this for yourself, not for others: "Let go and let God." Pray everyday. Pray:

"Lord, show me how to let go of fear, anger, and anxiety. Show me. I desire to let go."

Practice this on a daily basis. When offenses come, say:

"I choose to walk in love. I cast down this evil imagination. I forgive the person, the situation."

We've got to walk in love. The Bible tells us to be tenderhearted. If you have the nature of God, you have the capacity to forgive. Whether you choose to or not is between you and God.

Chapter Three

The Stages of Recovery

All of us get knocked down in life;
winners manage not to get knocked-out!

The recovery process varies from one loss to another, depending on the intensity of feelings that were connected to the individual or item that was lost. Also, the amount of time it takes to recover, which is the duration of the healing process, differs in each case. The greater the loss, the more intense your feelings are going to be and the more pronounced each stage of your recovery. The time it takes to pass from one stage of recovery to the next depends on your willingness to want to be healed.

Regardless of your trauma, you will experience various stages of the recovery process before you are made whole.

The First Stages
The first level of recovery includes the stages of:

1) shock, 2) denial, and 3) numbness.

SHOCK

The first thing experienced when you have been wounded, whether physically, mentally, or emotionally, is shock. Shock is a condition that results after an event occurs as an unforeseen blow. Shock is the violent impact on the mind or emotions of an unexpected, overwhelming incident. When you're in shock, the mind cannot put the account of what has happened to you together with its own line of reasoning. Some of us have never progressed past the stage of shock.

DENIAL

Denial is the refusal to believe or accept that an overwhelming event has occurred. Denial is the process that is taking place when we say or act upon thoughts like, "I can't believe this is happening to me," or "This is not happening to me."

I remember when I lost my wife. I didn't want to believe that she was dead. I kept looking for her. Every night before I went to bed, I watched to see if she was going to walk through the door. I was in denial to an overwhelming reality in my life.

The mind does not progress when it is in denial. Unlike our physical bodies, our minds do not continue to grow and mature past the point of emotional damage, unless we get healed. The mind becomes retarded, which simply means "made slow," and we suffer from an inability to correctly assess our losses. In denial, we explain away the reality of injury, or we simply refuse to face it.

Our attempts to respond in an overly spiritual manner actually delay the healing process. We can exert tremendous mental energy in our efforts to be spiritual and strong about our losses, but proper healing will not take place any more than if we put a tiny bandage on a deadly, cancerous disease. Just because the overwhelming feelings of devastation are not as fresh in our minds as when we first received the blow does not mean that we have completely recovered. This is where a lot of us get fooled.

Most of us don't recognize emotional problems within our minds because we are in denial. We say, "I'm fine," but we have not allowed God to heal us of past hurts. The unhealed area of pain and injury is bound to come out in some way later in life as a character defect. You are on your way to making life miserable for someone at home, at work, at church, or anywhere that your injured soul gets jarred in the course of human contact.

Most of us don't get past denial. We can remain upon our emotional feet, standing in that stage of denial for as long as it takes for us to uncover and face the truth.

NUMBNESS

Numbness is a condition of deadness and insensibility. In the stage of numbness, you are either weakened or deprived of the power to experience your own feelings. Numbness is the body's natural protection against shock and pain. It acts as an anesthesia of sorts, which prevents the mind from grasping all the pain at one time.

When you have endured small hurts, your mind goes through the initial three stages (shock, denial, and numbness) relatively quickly, sometimes in a matter of minutes. But those of you whose minds (and souls) have suffered a deep wound will take much longer to progress through the three preliminary stages of recovery.

Numbness can often be mistaken for healing, or confused by onlookers as "inner strength." In our religiosity, many times we paste a smile upon our lips, stifle the cry of pain, and appear as icons of faith in God when, in actuality, we're in the stage of numbness; the reality of what has occurred simply hasn't hit us yet.

The Second Stages

The second season (stages) of recovery that the mind goes through are: 1) fear, 2) anger, and 3) depression.

FEAR

Fear manifests during recovery, because our base of security is shaken. Anytime you are hit with the unexpected or unfamiliar, a measure of fear will present itself. When loss is involved, you will be faced with the unforeseen image of your life that will be out of sync with your daily routine; that which gave comfort to you may now be missing. Your thoughts may center upon these words: "What do I do now?"

One must methodically assess every aspect of life affected by the sudden change or sudden loss. You may find yourself with new responsibilities which, previously, you stood upon another to fulfill. Now, you find yourself in the midst of processing your emotional pain, having to re-identify your own role in life.

ANGER

Good children do get angry. Even God's children get angry. But, it's how you process anger that's important. You should express the emotion of anger in an appropriate manner so that you can move beyond it. Holding anger inside is not appropriate. Process your anger -- never bury it. You need a constructive, positive way of releasing and dealing with anger so that you can lie down at night and sleep well. When we say, "forget it," we need to really forget it.

Anger is a feeling that results from injury or some kind of mistreatment that may be real or imagined. Anger can also be the result of a person's needs not getting met. Anger is a by-product of the law of cause and effect: something has caused the anger that you see in angry people.

There are many sources of our anger. We are angry about our losses. We are angry about what has been happening to us. We are angry about having to move, about money we may have lost, and about love that we might have lost or never had. We're angry about being a victim or about abuses we've suffered and we're angry with the insensitive person who has abused us.

Anger results when our passions are provoked. Anger is prolonged when we continue to focus our minds on the negative thoughts and images that are the source of our anger. This habit of mentally "playing back" the injury and abuse causes damage in the emotional realm. This is the thing that does the most damage in divorces, separations, and relational break-ups.

Do you realize the power of denial? You can deny what has happened to you and be separated from a man or a woman ten years, and your mind has the ability to thrust you into a sudden flashback. You can regress back to that stage of your emotional trauma, and guess what? You'll find yourself feeling the same way you did the day of that loss.

The human mind doesn't forget anything. Just because you cannot remember it, does not mean your mind has forgotten it. It's just this: when the mind deems that it cannot remember something, it drops it from the conscious to the subconscious. Sometimes you think you have forgotten something, but you haven't. Flashbacks indicate that it is still there, in your mind.

If left unchecked, anger will cause you to turn on yourself or turn on others. When anger is directed inwardly, it will work itself into depression and repression. When anger is turned outwardly, it manifests itself as unforgiveness and bitterness.

Anger is a raging fire. The same fire that heats your house can burn it down if that fire is out of control. In Proverbs 6:27, the wisdom of Solomon asks, "Can a man take fire to his bosom and not get burned?" In Ephesians 4:26, the Holy Ghost instructs us, "...Let not the sun go down on your wrath." God knows the devastating results of anger and He commands that you do not allow anger to stay in you or around you.

The effect of anger upon your health is extremely destructive. If you do not diffuse and release anger, it will work itself into your emotions and then into your flesh. Once it lodges in your physical body, it manifests itself as diseases, literally taking years off of your life. Cancer, arthritis, colitis, migraines, and a host of other physical ailments can often be attributed to anger that has been ignored.

Staying angry is like having your intestines filled with hydrochloric acid -- it will continually eat away at your insides and, eventually, something is going to be destroyed. The body dumps a load of adrenaline into your bloodstream when you get angry. This adrenaline gives you supernatural energy. It puts your body in such an "up" mode that, when mixed with anger, it may cause you to hurt someone. If you do not use wisdom in expressing your anger, you have the potential to kill someone. This is the primary reason parents should never discipline their children when they are angry.

Anger has to be redirected. Redirection requires that you channel the energy that has been awakened due to anger into something positive or productive. The damaging energy produced by your anger wants to consume something.

Anger, however, can be worked out of you. Angry people need to include physical activity (particularly, cardiovascular exercise) into their daily routine. This will serve as an outlet for destructive, pent-up emotions. You must take the initiative to remove anger; God is not going to do it for you. Anger is an emotion and, as such, must be harnessed and brought under discipline, for you must rule your spirit.

Learning to be slow to anger is a valid goal that is necessary for every Christian. "Wherefore, my beloved brethren, let every man be swift to hear, slow to speak, slow to wrath (anger, indignation, vengeance)" (James 1:19). Be honest. Does that sound like you?

Learning to avoid abusive behavior in expressing anger is another valid goal for every Christian. In other words, learn how to express anger without cursing; learn how to be angry without thinking about what you want to do to the person who made you angry.

Anger perpetuates itself if we continue to think about what provoked us. If you would just change the thoughts in your mind, you will not stay angry. Is that why the Bible tells us, "Whatsoever things are true, honest, just, pure, lovely...think on these things" (Philippians 4:8, paraphrased). Is that why Isaiah said that "...a mind stayed on Him (Jesus), He will keep in perfect peace" (Isaiah 26:3). How can you have the peace of God, without having the God of peace? His name is called Peace -- Jehovah Shalom. "Shalom" means "peace" in Hebrew. We never have too much peace in our lives, especially if we live in a traumatic, tumultuous, highly kinetic, effervescent, hustling-bustling metropolis (like Chicago, where I live) and work in a "people" job. On the contrary, that type of living brings a lot of stress and a lot of unsettling to our lives.

BITTERNESS

Don't be bitter; be better!

When a person gets angry and continues to dwell on his anger, the anger turns into bitterness. Bitterness says, "I didn't get revenge the way I wanted to." Bitterness makes you want to kill somebody (anger makes you want to whip somebody); and when you get mad, you just want to slap somebody. The Bible says don't even go to bed with anger inside of you (Ephesians 4:26).

Just because you cannot always feel your anger doesn't mean it's not there. Most folks with cancer do not always feel it. Demons can walk right in you and you probably won't know it. When you find out they are in you, it's usually because they've done some damage.

UNFORGIVENESS IS A SERIOUS OFFENSE. In the parable about the unforgiving servant, the Bible says, "And his lord was wroth and delivered him to the tormentors..." (Matthew 18:34). Jesus is talking to believers! We have a worse judgment, "For him that knows right and does wrong, shall be beaten with many stripes" (Luke 12:47, paraphrased). The one that did not know right and did wrong, the Lord says he will be beaten with few (Luke 12:48).

I cannot convey to you as one called to bring deliverance and healing to the Body of Christ how important this information is. Everything else is superficial if the areas of unforgiveness and bitterness are not dealt with. Whenever you have an opportunity to pray for someone, you ought to question them about the area of bitterness and unforgiveness. If they are not willing to forgive, there is not much with which you can agree with them in prayer.

DEPRESSION

Depression is nothing to play with. It is very important that you understand as much as you can about depression.

Depression is brought on by:

1) Suppressed anger,
2) Suppressed fear,
3) Grief over a lost loved one.

So, check this out: some people you see on the job (that mother, brother, sister, friend) that you have been wondering about, wondering why they are so hard to live with, unbeknownst to you, they may be dealing with some form of depression -- maybe triggered by a loss. Just to look at such people and their daily erratic behavior, you may not know what they are reacting to unless you take the time to ask some hard questions. Let's not become so turned off by a person's attitude that we stop caring. An individual's bad attitude is a signal of their pain, not an accusation against their personhood. Most people are too embarrassed to talk about their losses, so they will not readily communicate with you. They just bury their hurt and keep it inside, locked in the chambers of denial. However, their subconscious mind attempts to communicate through their abruptness, nastiness, and defensiveness.

There are an estimated 24 million people in this country suffering from some form of depression. Isn't that unfathomable? Doctors, psychologists, and the American Medical Association all concur that depression is an illness. If you are in deep states of clinical or manic depression, you have to be put on medicine. The medicine helps the brain secrete the hormones necessary to stabilize the detrimental chemicals your emotions are causing your body to release. Medication is necessary because in a depressive state, parts of the brain have stopped operating all together. When a doctor has clinically diagnosed depression, the afflicted person has to take prescribed medications that enable him to function at a parody of normalcy. But, all the medication in the world cannot remove the root of the anger -- that is still up to the individual.

Most people who have developed addictions (like alcoholics) are usually manic-depressive. They are trying to escape their depression. Dope, alcohol, and even sleep provide a means of escape from a litany of painful thoughts, which one's conscious cannot digest.

That brings us to the subject of why some people we know seem to be lazy. It may not be because they just want to sleep and that's it. They may be using sleep as a way of escape from dealing with the realities of life. Sleep is the brother of death. It provides us with another world in which the subconscious can attempt to process the inner turmoil through the avenue of dreams. The subconscious will attempt to bring the matter to a conclusion through symbolic dreams that "jump-start" the conscious mind -- similar to when you jump-start a battery. Dreams come to consciously make you think about things you don't want to think about. And when the subconscious is seeking escape, delusional dreams of grandeur will be contrived in a vain attempt to create a new reality in which to dwell.

Drugs also allow us to escape for a little while but, when they wear off, we come back to reality. Now, the problem is still there, plus, the complication of an addiction to the escape mechanism is added, which exacerbates the problems that you already have. Many people never come to a place of confrontation with the truth. But, in order to progress, you must examine the places of pain that you are trying to avoid.

Non-reconciled loneliness will lead a person to depression. Doctors refer to depression as mentally "hitting rock bottom." Depression, if not dealt with immediately, can mushroom into a serious mental illness. If there is a history of mental illness in your family, any form of depression demands immediate psychiatric care or professional counseling.

The length of time a person remains in depression depends on his personality. Depression is a natural feature in the grieving process; so, in times of grief, being depressed is not entirely a wrong response. It can be a time of rigorous self-evaluation that has been ordained of God. While you're having your little "rock-bottom" experience all alone, God takes advantage of the situation and allows you to examine yourself. The finger of blame for our lot in life that we may have been pointing at others comes to rest back on ourselves. Depression can be a time of challenge and awakening to what God is showing us about ourselves.

We cannot play with people in depression -- we have to be lovingly firm. Self-pity will have a person desiring to be pitied. We do need to love people but, at the same time, be firm and refuse to baby them. Care must also be taken not to send a person deeper into depression. Identify with what they are going through without pitying them. We must guide them through the path of self-discovery, without allowing them to build an island unto themselves.

The Book of Psalms reveals a lot of David's emotional up and down experiences. I don't know a man in the Bible that was more depressed than David. He was so depressed one day, the Bible says, "David encouraged himself in the Lord" (I Samuel 30:6). The Book of Psalms shows that we can be honest with our feelings in the Presence of God. God never said that our emotions were sinful. God has emotions. He gets angry, becomes jealous, becomes sickened, laughs and cries -- just as we do. We all have ups and downs. After all, we're made in "His Image."

In summation, some stages of depression can bring a temporary pause, peace of mind, and much needed rest. Sometimes God allows that season of depression, allowing us to rest, before we rust!

Repression shares a similarity with depression in that both deal with anger. Repression, however, is anger turned inward. Repression reduces your body's ability to defend itself from disease, stress, and fatigue. Repression is often the culprit in individuals that develop frequent colds and minor ailments, such as, headaches (particularly migraines), backaches, and constipation, all over aches, and those who are just plain sickly. Folks who are housing repression always seem to have something wrong with them. The body becomes stiffened and taunt as the result of repressed anger, and our nerves become frayed on the inside.

Most Americans suffer from repression, especially people in the work force whose jobs are stressful. These people think they have controlled and eliminated their anger; but the person who has the problem with repression needs their anger redirected. Repression can even cause us to develop insomnia, the inability to sleep or rest. This inability to get comfortable and go off to sleep is caused by not having dealt with the root of the problem. Repression is very dangerous and it can kill.

Where is Your Niche?

Some people are perfectionists as they attempt to repair the brokenness they feel inside, while others don't even realize that the problem is within their own hearts or choose to ignore it. This describes two extremes of the categories into which psychologists state everyone falls: being either neurotic or housing a character disorder.

NEUROTICISM

Neurotics are easy to work with in therapy because they assume total responsibility for their difficulty. Therefore, neurotics do realize that they are having problems. Most neurotic people will tell you, "I have a problem and I know I have a problem." In fact, a neurotic assumes too much responsibility. A neurotic individual is quick to assume guilt; and because of their drive for perfection and their need for approval, they exist as driven individuals who have a great challenge in ever coming to a place of relaxation and rest with who they really are.

CHARACTER DISORDERS

Individuals with character disorders do not assume enough responsibility. The person with a character disorder will lie to himself and others. They are impossible to work with in therapy because they don't see themselves as the problem. They see everyone else as the problem and they believe the world needs to change -- not them. They figure, "I'm alright and everybody else is crazy." These people can't see themselves because a demon has walked in and blinded them from seeing the source of their problem. They will point fingers at everyone around them but not at themselves.

People with character disorders have a track record of abusing people wherever they go. If you mention to them that they have abused others, they will deny it and say, "Oh, that person was blessed by meeting me. I allowed them to know me." People with serious character disorders are legends in their own minds and very few of them get help. With God, you cannot get His help until you admit that you have a problem.

The Last Stages

If you allow yourself to go through the first two stages of the healing process, the last stage will be to: understand, accept, and move on. In other words, you will say, "I understand now. I accept that it was a loss." You will understand why B.B. King sings, The Thrill Is Gone. You can sing, The Trauma is Gone. You are now able to cope and you're ready for love again.

Our mind accepts what life brings when it realizes that it is possible to go on after we have faced a loss. We can move on to the next change of life because we have survived.

Chapter Four

Emotional Hindrances to Recovery

God can only act
within our will!

Some people are thoroughly open and cooperative. They successfully complete the stages of recovery and come out totally healed. That, by no means, is the majority of us who suffer loss and experience trauma. On the road to recovery, most of us are thwarted because of obstacles along the way. However, the greatest obstacles that block our healing are our own negative emotions. Some of the emotional hindrances to recovery are: pride, shame, self-deception, loneliness, deception, emotional overload, chronic shock syndrome, and demonic mind control.

PRIDE

Pride is the tool the devil will use to keep from being discovered. Even when people ask you about a problem, pride will jump up and say, "No, I am not bothered with that. (I won't tell them anything. They will think I'm weak.) That is not bothering me." Pride will stop you from getting help. Anger gets you in trouble, but pride keeps you there. It is bad to be an angry person, but adding pride to your anger makes it worse. That is a combination that leaves you quite unteachable.

I wonder how many times you hear a sermon and you know God is talking to you through that preacher -- not only a sermon from your local pastor, but from anyone else that God may use. When the preacher makes an altar call for you to come forth and get healed, your pride may say, "If you get up, folks are going to know. Everybody's going to know that you have a problem with this." Guess what? They probably know already, whether you get the help or not. You aren't fooling anyone, not even yourself.

James 4:6 says, "God resists the proud". God may resist (oppose, contest against, counteract, confront, challenge) you, but God doesn't want you hurting. God will provide the help. So, when you're hurting, you have to get some help!

SHAME

Shame is when someone or something causes us disgrace. Shame produces a desire to hide. Shame makes you want to get under a rock or jump into a hole and move the opening. Shame makes you want to volunteer for the next space flight. Shame makes you want to go home, close the door, and never come out. Shame will hurt you so bad it will cause you to get in bed and never want to get up -- because of the pain and hurt. We have to acknowledge our shame and admit to it.

The first step toward recovery is refusing to accept what the devil wants to do -- which is to keep you right there in that shame. Shame is a very natural emotion, but it is not a permanent dwelling place. And, as long as you have emotions and have gone through any type of loss, hurt, or rejection, you will experience some shame.

SELF-DECEPTION

If you get caught up in shame on the way to recovery from an emotional wound, another diabolic doorway can open that leads to self-deception. Self-deception is a false belief concerning oneself. Self-deception is an outgrowth of rebellion and is rooted in rejection. Rebellion is when a person refuses to yield to valid authority. Self-deception decides, "no one will tell me what to do; I do as I please." This is a spirit. Everything we discussed up until now (and the emotional hindrances we will discuss) is connected to different demonic spirits.

Midway into a season of healing, it is possible to pick up all of these conditions and be stuck in that season. The loss perpetuated the hurt > The hurt opens the door to the shame > The shame opens the door to self-deception > Self-deception opens the door to more rejection > Rejection creates emptiness in one's life. Hungering for love, hungering for respect, hungering for honor, and hungering to be fulfilled -- self-deception leaves behind you a trail of burned down bridges while a spirit is actually exploiting you through your mind.

There is a pastor in a certain city that God wanted me to minister to and I tried intensely to get to him for a long time. But, as I discovered later, a spirit of deception told him, "You don't need to talk to Apostle. You're alright." He experienced the turmoil and division in his church and in his personal life that God wanted him to avoid. He was wounding people all around that city, because hurt people hurt other people. He got all messed up. He could have avoided all of that if he would have just allowed the person that God sent to minister to him access to his heart. God sent me, as an Apostle, to that city, and I knew this man's problems from years past; but self-deception told him that he was all right. He couldn't yield. As a result of it, he is now reaping the fruit of his self-deception.

Will you allow someone to speak into your life, or will you cling to a deception? People, who think they are right, and most "know-it-alls," have this problem -- those "got-to-be-right-all-the-time" people. They will cling to a self-deception because it makes them feel good, while they could very well be burning up the connections that would lead to their healing.

LONELINESS

I do not care how saved you are, you will become lonely. If you are single, you will become lonely for companionship. Society puts pressure on folks to "have somebody in their lives." Once you have reached the chronological age of maturity, the pressures of society begin to meddle in your affairs. "Aren't you married yet? Don't you have children yet? How old did you say you were?" Single people will feel that pressure. Sometimes because of this pressure, you don't want to tell anyone your age.

Thanksgiving and Christmas holidays are seasons where the police say many people take their lives, simply because of loneliness. You can be married and be lonely, or you can be in a room full of people and still be lonely. If a person is married and lonely, somebody is not doing his or her job. It is your job to make your spouse feel that they are important. Loneliness is a problem primarily among women. Women have to be constantly affirmed. You can be in a relationship with a love-starved person, and they will "get on your nerves," because whatever you do for them is never enough. You tell them you love them, you hug them, you kiss them, you make love to them for three hours, but, still, it is not enough.

If you are in a relationship with a love-starved person, you need to get some understanding about things, such as, what you are capable of doing and what you are not capable of doing. Because if you don't get an understanding, that person will feel as if they are not valuable or that you have rejected them. They may become angry and you will have to deal with that anger.

People start feeling lonely when they are overly in tune to their emotions. Emotionally, there are three things that all of us need and that is:

To give love;
To receive love; and
Acceptance.

When people don't feel loved or when they don't feel valuable, then they may begin to feel lonely. Or, if spouses neglect their duties, loneliness sets in. Loneliness is an absence of direction, not an absence of affection. In other words, you don't know what to do with yourself when you are lonely. Some of us do not realize that it is loneliness that we are feeling; but the more you figure you don't know what to do, the lonelier you become.

When in love, the first stages are when you let down your legal boundaries -- your little emotional barriers. All of us have little emotional idiosyncrasies with which we keep people off of us...especially if we've been wounded before. But, when you're in love, your barriers should come down. You usually fall in love when you have made up your mind that you are through being lonely -- you are tired of being lonely. Some folks who fall in love all the time have a serious problem with loneliness. "I'm lonely, so will you love me? Please?" If you buy him a candy bar, he'll say, "I think I love you." You don't love him and he doesn't love you. One of you was just hungry! So, don't get into dire straits over something that's really nothing and don't get desperate.

Uncontrolled anger will lead to insanity!

THE ELIJAH SYNDROME

Most people who are hurt, lonely, broken-hearted, shamed, repressed, or depressed go through what I call "The Elijah Syndrome." I Kings 19:10 says:

> *"And he said, I've been very jealous for the Lord God or Hosts for the children of Israel have forsaken Thy covenant, thrown down Thy altars, and slain Thy prophets with the sword; and I, even I only am left and they seek my life to take it away."*

This is the "I'm-all-alone complaining demon." The devil wants all of us to feel that no one else is "going through" but us. Our problems seem so unique. God told Elijah that he had seven thousand people left and to stop the "pity-party."

All of us go through things. However, we do not want to believe that other people are going through things, too. Many times, as saints of God, we don't show what we go through on our countenance, because we have been told we are to be positive at all times. We should be positive because we have the Holy Ghost. He will keep us positive and keep us with a good mental attitude, especially if we stay around strong people. The truth is we do go through things, even with the Holy Ghost, but He will strengthen us on our way through and deliver us -- mind, soul, and body.

DECEPTION

Proverbs (4:23) says, *"Guard your heart for out of it comes the issues of life."* One thing that we must guard our hearts against on the road to recovery is deception, which comes in three stages.

Stage One:
Your Sensitivity to a Sin Wears Down

Satan likes to use things that wear down your conscience in order to bring deception. In other words, when you are in sin for so long, you no longer have the conviction that you once had about that sin. It does not bother you as much as it used to. You can become insensitive to sexual sins if you allow yourself to watch lewd, sensual, and erotic programs on TV. This will wear down your spiritual conscience to the point where you begin to think, "That isn't so bad."

The first time you see a man and woman making love on TV, on a movie screen, or in a porno movie, you say, "Oh, man! Those folks ought to be ashamed of themselves." And the first time you saw somebody naked, your reaction was much stronger than it is now. But the more nudity you see, the less it bothers you, because the devil likes to wear down your conscience, making it easy to be deceived into committing sin.

Stage Two:
You Build a Foundation for Immoral Behavior

Satan and demons are strategists. They will observe your reaction to sin. If you are not casting down ungodly imaginations, then you are receiving their input and, in their estimation, you like it. So, they will slip another image in there on you. As you allow sin to go unrestrained, it enters your conscience because the image starts to create desire. Now, the pornographic movies you look at don't offend you any longer; now, you want to carry out the act. You will find some of the weirdest people watching dirty movies and then they will carry out what they see.

Stage Three:
Isolation

Never let the devil lead you to believe that you don't need anyone and that God just wants you to be quiet. Although every man should bear his own burden, we are also called to "bear one another's burdens" (Galatians 6:2).

Some people have demons and Satan tells them, "This is just your personal business and what you do isn't anyone else's business. This is a private matter between you and whomever." That philosophy will kill you. That philosophy is what has our mental institutions overflowing and has caused people to take guns to their heads, blowing out their brains and blowing away others. When your emotions become frayed and overworked, they are like an overloaded socket or breaker-box. You will blow a fuse. When you blow a fuse emotionally, it is called having a "nervous breakdown." That is the emotion's way of saying, "This is too much. I can't take it anymore."

EMOTIONAL OVERLOAD

You cannot fool the mind. When you start trying to put too much on the mind, the mind says, "I'm shutting down." Do you know what is happening? Long before the mind starts shutting down, it stops cooperating with you. The mind will start to say, "I won't receive anymore information" and you will start to have memory problems: "I can't remember my phone number, and I can't remember my address. What is my name? Where do I live?" The simple information that is stored in your mind cannot be recalled. The mind has become overloaded and you are on the road to a nervous breakdown. You are on your way to a mental institution and to your own custom-made straight jacket. Folks are going to lock you up.

When we experience mood swings – serious mood swings – they always indicate demonic activity. Up, down, up, down: "I love Jesus; I don't know if I love Him. I'm an evangelist; I'm a prophet; I'm a pastor; I'm a teacher; I'm just a member." There continues to be much inner turmoil in your emotions.

CHRONIC SHOCK SYNDROME

Chronic shock syndrome works like this: You may have

been involved in a traumatic event and your emotions were so overwhelmed that you go into emotional shock. As a result, you turn off your emotions and become numb. This is a defense mechanism that God has given you to help you cope with your traumatic events. Later, perhaps, the numbness subsides and your emotions begin to come back. This is an important tie to process your intense feelings. You will ask questions like, "Why did this happen to me? Was it my fault? Will it ever happen again?"

You're going through enough stuff. There's no sense in killing yourself and kicking yourself. Do you realize a lot of the things that are whipping you today aren't the devil? It's God "tightening you up" because you're being judged. It's you kicking yourself in the butt because you failed to act like Christ. How can you call yourself a Christian when you don't act like the person you are following? Acting like Jesus is one indication that you are maturing in Him.

Personally, I have a lot to be mad about. I have a lot to hate people about. But, I refuse to sit and dwell on it. "For as a man thinketh in his heart, so is he" (Proverbs 23:7). You are the total sum of your thoughts. If your mind is on mess, what kind of person are you: a messed-up person. If your mind is on anger, you are an angry person. If your mind is on revenge all the time, you are a revengeful person. If you are bitter, that says that you are angry because you didn't get revenge.

DEMONIC MIND CONTROL

Satan wants you to be quiet about things that have you messed up. There are closet homosexuals, pedophiles, and dope addicts that are tormented in their minds through a demonic appetite that is seeking to be quenched.

Satan will walk into an area of your life where you have been wounded. His strategy is to attempt to keep you wounded or to bring about some type of mental retardation in connection with that wounded area. Your logic and your ability to rationalize in that area will be off and out of balance. When things are not balanced, you can expect some heresy and excess, some demonic activity and some demonic doctrines.

The devil's objective is to make you dull of comprehension in the areas in which you have been wounded. Something that is really simple, like telling someone whom you have hurt that you are sorry, is no longer that simple to a person who has been wounded.

The attempt to keep you "stuck" usually happens midway in a season, through a spirit. Satan tries (and is usually quite successful) to come during a season of transition and hurt. I don't know a person yet who has been in a prolonged season of hurt that does not have a spirit in them that has them bound in a certain area, preventing their growth. As a result of this, we have people sitting in church who really cannot understand or rightfully divide the Word of Truth. They cannot comprehend and neither can they hold onto the Word. There are people who cannot even remember Scriptures. Demons will do this to your mind.

How many people do you know (and you may be one of them) who says, "I can't remember Scriptures. I can't memorize the words." You had no problem memorizing all of those dirty lyrics and those songs you used to sing. What's the difference between a lyric and a Psalm? Well, why don't you memorize the Book of Psalms? It's a collection of songs! Why…because these spirits are attempting to control your mind.

Let me put it another way: Demonic spirits try to come in and stunt your growth or change your personality. Satan knows he cannot make a man, but if he can control one, it is like making one. In every traumatic situation you've gone through, there has been a spirit present to keep you bound to that memory and to that hurt. It might be feelings of rejection and/or fear. In every traumatic situation you have gone through, there has been a spirit present to make sure you were tormented in your mind.

Believe me when I tell you this: the Lord said to me, "Cliff, this is a spirit called "mind control." Psychologists, as well as doctors, know about the stem at the base of the head that leads to the brain. Whoever has access to the brain stem controls the whole mind. Just like there was fighting in the Persian Gulf for control of oil, Satan says, "If I can just control this area (of the brain), I can control the whole person."

Gaining control of your mind is possible, especially since most people don't even know who they really are. We've grown up with mindsets – programmed thoughts, superficial reactions, and interactions with everything in which we come in contact. So, Satan will attempt to control the mind by demon oppression.

A lot of us cannot discern when people are oppressed of the devil. It doesn't mean that they are demon possessed, and it doesn't mean that they don't love God.

I was praying for a person who was oppressed in this area. The Lord had me to address the spirit of mind control in this individual. The Holy Spirit said, "Put your hand at the base of the person's brain and in the Name of Jesus say, 'I bind that spirit of mind control. Set this person free in Jesus' Name.'" You would have thought a water hydrant had burst in this person's mouth. If you have not seen people getting purged and delivered from spirits, imagine a fire hydrant bursting. I said, "God in Heaven." It smelled so bad while the person was being delivered that had to leave out of the washroom after I finished praying for this person. This person literally began filling up the commode. There were so many unclean spirits, and then came the strongman, being purged right there.

Did you not know that Satan is very crafty? I want you to understand his craftiness. There is no depth too low for him to stoop. So, keep this in mind. There are three times when the devil tries to attack you:

At the birth of something big,
When you wait until the last minute to do something, *and*
When you are at your most vulnerable state.

The third occasion when the devil is most likely to attack you – when you are most vulnerable – is usually when those suffering loss, grief, and other traumatic situations are mercilessly attacked by the devil. It is the devil's intention to smear your name and do you harm. He is out to keep you from becoming all you are called to be. But, once you understand Satan's strategies and purpose in your heart to live by the Word of God, Satan is rendered powerless in your life. You are resisting the devil and you better believe that he's going to flee!

Chapter Five

More on Shame

Bad things do happen to good people.

Will this be a stepping stone or a tombstone?

"For your shame, ye shall have double!   (Isaiah 61:7)

Shame is a big problem among my people...my black people...as a result of institutionalized and internalized degradation of our personhood. This particular kind of shame is more prevalent among black people than any other people on the face of the earth. Some of us are ashamed of being black or are ashamed of our various skin complexions. Some of us are ashamed because we don't like our features. We have been made to be ashamed of our big lips, our broad noses, and our big hips. We are ashamed because we do not have enough education and because we have been poor too long. We are ashamed of our ancestors and ashamed of the yoke of slavery that was unjustly placed upon their shoulders.

We are ashamed of the blatant racism that fuels the KKK and others whose white hoods cannot be seen by the naked eye but are discerned in our workplaces, our neighborhoods, our stores and, yes, even within our churches. We have been hurt, embarrassed, and ridiculed in our impoverished condition.

When the controlling forces behind media begin to label "beautiful" people, they rarely show black people. We have bought into that lie to the point of thinking that if we don't bleach our hair, we're not pretty. Blonde hair is beautiful upon those whom God intended it to be. Blonde hair is natural to those who are born with it. I've seen it on dogs and I can show you a pony with a blonde tail. It is beautiful. What I'm trying to get you to understand is that God knows what He's doing, but society has disgraced the Black race. And, in so many instances, our own brothers and sisters arose and "dissed" (disrespected, disgraced, discouraged...) us, too.

Black people are living under an onslaught of shame. We are ashamed of who we are and we're ashamed of our culture. Other cultures don't have a problem telling you what they eat. Italians are proud of their spaghetti, and Jewish people have no problem in telling you that they eat lochs and bagels. But, black people, you don't even want to tell people that you eat cornbread and black-eyed peas. You don't want to tell anyone that you had some neck bones for dinner. You're ashamed of being who you are. So, when you get around a certain group of people, you try to be what you think they will accept. You are probably going through some form of shame right now as you are reading this.

I know a lot of black men who are going through some shame because they don't think they are intelligent enough to successfully compete with other men. Our own black women are capable of putting tremendous pressure on our men which can be as destructive as the most racist elements in our society.

Women: your men are listening to you when you say, "I just wish we could afford a better house. I wish we could afford a better car." Sometimes the shame you have caused your husband to feel affects his self-image. In some instances, he has to work hard just to cover his shame, or he may stay away from home because he is ashamed. You remind him of what he is not. Whether this is done publicly or privately, these types of comparisons will cause problems in a marriage, because a man's self-esteem is tied into what he has.

Men are competitive by nature. When they get together, they immediately start discussing "things." "Well, ha-ha, the Lord blessed me and I just got a brand new so and so." "And, you know, I just moved into an eight-bedroom condo in a very exclusive area." "And, while we're on the subject, I'm getting ready to go and do some shopping on North Michigan Avenue...there's a sale on at Brooks Brothers and Armani suits are on sale as well, you know...." Yeah, right! In reality, this same brother has so little money, he can't pay anyone; he can't even pay attention. He's shopping at B.B.'s all right, that is, Big Ben's or even the Unique Thrift Store. So, we see that some men avoid the truth just not to be put to shame.

Everyone can identify with being made to feel ashamed. Imagine this: you just earned your GED, and all the other folks are talking about what university they went to and how they graduated and received degrees. That might cause you to move into shame. You could very well be mopping the floors at the school that you attended to get your GED and feeling that you were doing just fine. As you are happy and pleased with your accomplishments – and rightfully so – you share them with others: "You know, last year, I just completed my GED." They may say, "You mean to tell me that all you've got is a GED? I thought you at least had your Master's degree!" How do you feel about yourself then? Shame! Shame! Shame!

It is no wonder that many people today don't really love themselves. If you are a person who is severely overweight, you are going through some shame. You are not going to admit it, but this is a society that is very "eye" conscious. If you are a larger person, the society that we live in makes you feel that you are ugly, and categorizing you in that way causes a sense of shame.

If you are a woman, there may have been men that made you feel ashamed. Personally, I do not see how a woman can allow a man to make her feel ashamed. Did you not know that before a person can put together a masterpiece, they always have to have a rough draft. So, when God made man, He made a rough draft. First, you make the rough draft, and then you make the masterpiece. The man was the rough draft and you, women, are the masterpiece – you are the true work of art!

You may also experience shame in your mind because you do not have what you want or what others have.

Some of you are happily married but concerned about what others think about your spouse. Wives heard someone saying, "Child, he sho' is ugly. I can't believe you married that man!" They are out to make you feel ashamed. Honey, listen: forget those folks! If you cut that man loose, eight "Sapphires" will be waiting to grab him up! They do not care what he looks like if he's bringing that "pretty money" home! What would you rather have…a pretty boy with no money or a multi-millionaire looking like a gorilla? If you have that much money, you can put a mask on a gorilla!!!

Every person I have ministered to with problems in the area of shame had one common characteristic – they were killing themselves. They did not know when to slow down, or when to go to bed, or when to come off their jobs (working long hours). They were not eating properly; they were not getting enough exercise; they were up late at night; and up early in the morning. They were self-destructing in a vain attempt to break the shackles of shame to which they had become enslaved.

Most people who are working too hard have a mental disorder. You may not deem what you are doing as a mental disorder, but you do have one. Shame tells you to work your way into acceptability. You work hard to be attractive, to be powerful, and to make lots of money. You work very hard to make people like you. It is so important for people to like you because you are living for other people's love.

Remember, the two types of people we spoke about earlier: neurotics and individuals that have a character disorder. Both of these people will self-destruct if they do not get some help.

Shamed people will allow others to disrespect them; or, the other extreme, they will insult and hurt themselves to keep others from hurting them first. They will put themselves down all the time with derogatory statements about themselves, like, "You know I'm stupid, so give me a break." "You know I'm nothing but a slob." "That's why this food is all over me. I'm just sloppy."

Most people who are in a state of shame look for someone

to make them feel good. Shamed women will seek approval, even to the point of becoming whores, just so someone will tell them they look good or are doing something right. They will allow themselves to be used like a doormat. Sometimes people can be in a state of shame for so long that they are thirsty and hungry for the affirmation of the opposite sex, and they will do anything humanly possible to attain affirmation.

Shame makes you apologize for hurt. There will be people to whom God will send to you for the purpose of talking about your problems. If you are in shame, you approach them by saying, "I'm so sorry to bother you about this. I know that I'm stupid. I know that this doesn't make any sense, but, please, can you give me a little bit of your time?" "This isn't real important, but, please, can you talk to me?" You are apologizing for your shame. "I know I should know better. I know I should read more. I know I should fast more. But, can you please share some time with me?" You continue apologizing for your shame. Have you ever been in that state?

Chapter Six

The Pain of Shame

When experiencing shame, there is always some form of pain that is being soothed and anesthetized usually by some form of false outlet. If you're hurting, admit it. To feel pain after a loss is normal; to feel pain after a loss is natural; to feel pain after a loss is proof that you are alive. Although your pain may frighten you, or make you feel uncomfortable (and it should), you should lean into your pain. Your pain is not a bottomless pit. You will always feel pain, but you must allow pain to have its way in your life. It's an important part of the healing process that you may need to deal with. Feel the hurt and don't deny it or cover it up. You are going to hurt for a while. Allow yourself to be in pain. See it as pain, not as hurting. Trust in the process of recovery.

I have been shamed, and it has been painful. When others do not live up to your own expectations, you can go through shame. When life does not work out for you like you have envisioned, you can go through shame. What if one of your little girlfriends or boyfriends that you grew up with comes by and tells you about all they have and all they are doing? That can bring shame. It makes you think about your little, one room apartment. You don't even want to tell folks what you're driving. They'll ask you, "So, what are you driving now?" Because you're so ashamed, you don't want to tell them the truth, but you don't want to lie either; so, you'll just say, "Oh, bless the Lord, the Lord's been good." You can have shame because of failures in your life...there's something you didn't live up to. There can be family secrets that bring shame in your life. Parental rejection can cause you to have shame. Your parents may have said, "I don't know why I had you. You're stupid." (That sounds like the parent is the one stupid, not the child!) And, all of this shame brings pain.

I know of some "stupid" parents who bring painful shame to their children. There was a woman in our church that spoke of her shame. She said she overheard her father talking to her mother, saying that he did not know why a particular boy was around her because he knew that she was ugly, and the boy must have only wanted "what's between her legs." She heard her Daddy call her black, and nappy-headed, and ugly. His statements took her for a loop; she underwent shame and great pain, because the shame came from those she loved the most and who were supposed to be her protection. Some of us grow up in homes where our parents prefer one child over the other because one is fair-skinned, or because one is thinner, or because one is smarter, or because one is more athletic. Did you not know that such things cause some shame that makes you feel that you are not good enough? Such feelings can lead to low self-esteem.

Abuse can create shame. Abuse is painful by its very nature, and the shame associated with it brings unbearable pain. If you have gone through a divorce, if you have gone through a separation, if you have gone through an untimely break-up, if somebody "dissed you," somebody left you, or somebody abandoned you – you have gone through shame. The women who have had abortions have gone through shame. The devil will white-wash you with a spirit of guilt and say, "Some Christian you are. You killed that baby. How old would that baby have been today? I wonder if it were a boy? Who'd he look like? (Or, if it were a girl) Who would she look like?"

I know I have gone through this kind of shame and God is healing me. Just when God is healing you in an area, watch the devil try to pull the scab off of your wound. But, just when I think I'm getting healed, somebody will walk up to me and say, "Hey, Brother Turner, I heard your wife left you." We must learn to ignore people, laugh it off, and get our healing!

I will be first to tell you that shame is an area in which God had to deal with me. When I went through the pain of losing my first wife, and when I went through the pain of a divorce, it shocked me. God showed me that I was going through shame. I was saying, "God, how can I face my church? How can I face my children? How can I go across the country when I've been from one end of the nation to the next preaching on family? How can I do this?" God said, "Square your shoulders back, hold your head up. You've been knocked down, but you've not been knocked out."

I know what shame is. I said, "Lord, will I ever lift up my head again? Lord, will I ever have the joy of my salvation restored again? Lord, will I ever know what it's like to be happily married again? Will I ever know what it's like to be in bed with a godly woman who loves Jesus and loves her man?" I am telling you what my mind was going through. The mind will play games with you. You may be thinking about one thing, and then, all of a sudden, the mind goes back to that pain.

They tell me that the tongue always goes back to the place of the missing tooth; and, in like manner, your mind goes back to its pain. I can be minding my own business watching TV and then all of a sudden, my mind wanders back to that pain. When I'm at a movie theater, looking at a good movie, and enjoying it, my mind goes back to the pain. Among the saints, fellowshipping, right in the middle of it, my mind goes back to the pain. Wait!!! Enough is enough! I asked the Lord about it, and He said, "Cliff, you have not allowed yourself to be vulnerable; open up and let My healing power heal that thing." He said, "You have not allowed yourself to go through the seasons of healing. You have prolonged your own misery."

What can you do with shame? Get rid of it! You did not come into things overnight. You will not come out of things overnight." "First the blade, then the ear, then the corn" (Mark 4:28, paraphrased). Healing starts the moment you have the attitude to want it. You will not receive your healing at all until you have the attitude of wanting to be healed.

Just as much as you have experienced shame, you need to ask the Holy Spirit, "Who have I put to shame?" You need to get before God and ask for forgiveness, because you will "reap what you sow" (Galatians 6:7, paraphrased). It just becomes a vicious cycle. When you put somebody to shame, God allows someone to shame you. Now you become angry and you put somebody else to shame; it is worse this time. The harvest of a seed always comes back multiplied. God allows somebody to shame you more, and the shame you inflict will spiral up more and more, until the devil will, ultimately, have you behaving coldly and insensitively to others. In each bad experience, the devil tries to numb your emotions so that you no longer care about anyone or anything. If this is the case with you, then you have allowed yourself to go too far and too long without help. Now, you need emergency help. After you receive that help, you will need to get the Scriptures and meditate upon them.

Chapter Seven

Shame in Love and Sex

Shame will put a wedge in relationships. You will not be able to be intimate with people or with God because you've undergone some shame. Shame always brings a feeling of being exposed. Shame leads you to push away and then to hold back. Shame says someone else deserves to have his or her needs met, but not yours. Shame will tell you, "You're not good enough for this." Shame will tell you, "You're not like those people."

Shame defies emotional closeness with people. When a person has gone through shame, it becomes a barrier to intimacy with friends, family, your spouse, and even God. A woman who has been whorish during a season of her life, who has been sleeping with a lot of men, may not want sex with her own husband, because she's still going through shame. When a woman has had a lot of premarital sex problems and hasn't gotten healed from it, she'll never be a good sex partner with you. She's got to get rid of that shame to be free sexually, to be a wife to you. It isn't because she's not a good sex partner. I've had some husbands come to me and say, "Apostle, my wife is not very good in bed." I heard a joke about that. The other guy said, "Oh, you're wrong about that!"

If your wife isn't a very good lover, it's not because she doesn't have the ability to be, but there is a barrier there, a wedge. And, it's not just in women. Sisters, every man wants to believe that he's "Super-Stud" with his wife. The greatest thing that you can do for your husband while he's making love to you is to let him believe that he's "wonderful." "Oh, man of God, what manner of man is this?" "Oh, you powerful brute, you! My neck was bothering me. Now, my neck is no longer stiff; in fact, I can see on top of the house right now."

There are a lot of men undergoing therapy today because their wives turned them down. When women embarrass their husbands sexually, these men will suffer from areas of impotence where they actually become unable to perform.

A woman's pelvic area and her mind are connected. When the mind is okay, the other area will be okay, too. I have already told the men that I minister to that you make love to a woman's mind before you make love to her body. And you will know what she's thinking about you. You'll know how she feels about you when you begin to make love to her.

A man's ability to perform sexually is also linked to his mind. When his mind has been scarred, it affects him. When a man doesn't want to make love to a woman, he can't stand her. You don't ever want to get your husband in that kind of a condition because when your sex life is damaged, it's hard to repair. When a man gets damaged (in his ego), his lower parts will not perform. I know men that were healthy. They were making love to their wives until their wives said something that turned them off. They went from "Long-John Silver" to "Pee-Wee" in the twinkling of an eye!

Shame defies emotional closeness with people. You wonder why you can't get close to some people? You're full of shame. People who are shamed won't let others get close to them. You can be married to them and they still won't let you get close to them. As corny and as crazy as it sounds, I've found this to be true, even between husbands and wives with their children. You may have parents that keep "dissing you" -- putting you at a distance; they're not close to you at all. Sister's, you've got daughters that can't get close to you. It might be because they've undergone some shame. I found out that when mothers complain about their children during pregnancy, that child picks that thing up in the womb and that child will not be close to that mother. Don't ever complain about your child. Just like John the Baptist in the womb heard the declaration about Jesus and leaped in Elizabeth's womb, likewise, your children have heard your declarations and they leaped up or retreated away from a close relationship with you. There are proven methods (one called the "Suzuki" method) where a mother starts speaking to her child yet in the womb: "You're going to be a great artist," or "You're going to be a powerful man or woman of God." "You're going to play a violin," or "You're going to be an accomplished pianist." And the child comes out of the womb looking for a piano.

Chapter Eight

Emotional Disorders That Can Have You Bound

Half the people you are angry with don't know it;

the other half don't care ...

so, who's really getting hurt here?

There are two things that abort healing and deliverance in your life: anger (which was covered in Chapter Three) and unforgiveness. Unforgiveness leads to blame and guilt. You cannot afford to have any of these in you and expect to receive God's healing power or God's delivering power.

ANGER

Anger will serve as a circuit breaker to keep you from getting your healing and deliverance. Anger tells us that something is wrong and signals that we are in danger of losing something that matters to us. We need to respond to danger, but we must not sin as we attempt to resolve our problems. It's amazing that "danger" and "anger" are spelled so similarly, with the exception of one letter "D."

God tells us what to do with anger. Anger is just as much as an emotion as love is. But, it is important how you process anger. The Bible says, "Don't let the sun go down on your wrath" (Ephesians 4:26). Get it out of your life! God knows the devastating effects anger can have on you emotionally as well as physically. Anger and unforgiveness will abort any great move of God in a person's life, including their healing.

Remember again the story in the Gospel of Mark, Chapter 5, about the Gadarenian demoniac. People said he was crazy. Jesus never spoke to him; but He spoke to the spirits. Jesus realized the man could not comprehend or receive anything in the natural until he was delivered from those spirits. This is what I see in churches today. It doesn't matter how many revivals you run; the people are bound. First, cast the spirits out of them, then they will be able to understand. These spirits keep people from understanding. These spirits keep people from relating and from receiving their healing. This is what you need to know and this is what is not being taught in many of our Word churches, because many of the teachers lack the experience.

I promise that the devil is going to fight you about the knowledge you receive through this book. You do well not to whisper wisdom in the ear of a fool. "For the natural man receives not the things of God, neither can he know them for they are spiritually discerned" (I Corinthians 2:14).

A misunderstanding of how a Christian should deal with anger may keep you from expressing genuine forgiveness toward other people. There's more to it than just saying, "I forgive you." You were hurt, you hid the pain, and the pain led you to anger. You felt the anger, but denied it. You voiced the words of "forgiveness," but you skipped the acknowledgement of what really happened. Forgiveness has not yet occurred. Like sin, you've got to confess it, release it, and forget it.

Unforgiveness, like anger, is a spiritual circuit breaker. Together, unforgiveness and anger block, abort, circumvent, and undermine healing and deliverance in anybody's life. If you have anger and unforgiveness in your life, I promise you that you haven't gone very far in God at all.

My experience with people holding anger and unforgiveness has been that they aren't even in a spiritual condition to comprehend the things of God. Anger is a fruit of the flesh. How can you be in the spirit and be in the flesh?

UNFORGIVENESS

A lot of diseases are connected with the mind: Psychosomatic. I've discovered that most people who hold grudges, aughts, unforgiveness, and hatred have cancers like you wouldn't believe. Most people that I know who have unforgiveness and bitterness in their lives report of having unbelievable arthritic conditions and brittle bones. The Lord told me to emphasize that many of His people are suffering from "psychotic/ psychosomatic conditions" because of their inability to trust and the inability to forgive.

Forgiveness means to put away. It's a release of a debt. You are chained to whomever you don't forgive and you are emotionally chained to the offense that they have committed. The person could have gotten saved and have gone on to be with the Lord, and here you are still lingering back in the year when that person offended you. You will never progress physically, and God knows you won't progress spiritually with unforgiveness in your life.

Unforgiveness will kill you. Forgiveness means giving up the right to review and giving up the right to seek revenge.

You choose to give up the right to get even. When you don't choose to do that, unforgiveness turns to bitterness.

Bitterness means, "I didn't get revenge." When people are bitter, it's because something happened to them and they have allowed it to fester to a point where they want revenge. The Bible warns you in Hebrews about what a root of bitterness will do. It says that it will grow and defile you (Hebrews 12:15).

Unforgiveness is sin. You don't know, beloved, the things that you open yourself up to when you're in sin. You may try to pray for a person, but if that person refuses to forgive, that person is in sin, and you might as well tell them that they are a coming attraction in hell. It's because when we refuse to forgive, we deny the very nature of God in us.

Unforgiveness is dangerous because it will abort every healing and every other spiritual move in your life. Satan wants to convince us that something someone did or neglected to do gives us license to hold an aught. He makes your problem seem so unique as if no one has ever gone through what you're going through. He tries to make you feel as if nobody has been hurt like you've been hurt. Who has been hurt more than Jesus has? If He can forgive and His Spirit is in you, why don't you act like your Big Brother, Jesus? When we deny that we can forgive, then we, as Christians, become hypocrites. God does not say that to an unbeliever because an unbeliever doesn't have the capacity to love like Jesus.

BLAME AND GUILT

You will find people who have not forgiven are blaming.

"If I hadn't been with him/her, this would not have happened." While you are in the blaming cycle, you run right into guilt and even self-condemnation. Blame and guilt are flip sides of the same coin. Both are a waste of time and energy. You ought to be too busy to try to get even. Negative thinking is not good. Negative thinking is mental malpractice. It is impossible to let go of a bad relationship when you are constantly seeing yourself as a victim. When you see yourself as a victim, that means that you're still chained. Let go of failure, blame, guilt, and start adopting attitudes that move you forward to get on with your life.

Blame and guilt will distract you from your real purpose in God's kingdom. Accept where you are and start building a new, fulfilling life in Christ right there. Some of us can get healed by reading good therapeutic books; some can receive our healing by going to counseling; some of us can get our healing by simply talking with trusted, godly friends. "...(Your) inheritance (is) among them that are sanctified "(Acts 20:32). The Bible also says, "There's safety in a multitude of (godly) counselors..." (Proverbs 11:14, 24:6, Psalm 1:1). Worldly people have worldly wisdom. If you just talk to some of your (worldly) friends, they will side with you because of nepotism. They will not be very objective, or even biased.

Guilt is an act of your own will. Guilt is 100% pure poison. "Whose report are you going to believe?" (Isaiah 53:1, paraphrased). Are you going to believe God's report, or are you going to believe the devil's report as he whispers things to you night and day?

MINISTRY

I would suggest if you are going to minister to people with these emotional problems, this is one of the first things I'd ask them besides, "Are you saved?" Ask them, "Is there anyone against whom you are holding an aught? Is there any unforgiveness in your heart?" Ask them to be honest, because anger and unforgiveness serve as circuit breakers and hinder any prayer you pray for anyone.

When you're praying for people who don't seem to be responding to your prayers, the devil will say, "See, you don't have any power." But, that person may have unforgiveness in their heart. You'd also do well to ask the Holy Spirit to help you look within your heart and see if you have any unforgiveness.

When you're going through an emotional crisis, I don't care how long it's been from the initial offense, or how long it's lasted – you're mentally crippled. So, if your emotions have been disturbed and violated, how will your response be to people? A lot of us continue to have character defects in our lives today that we've never communicated to anyone. If people don't know what you're going through (from a professional standpoint), and if people can't discern what season you're in, you're going to come off as being a 100% "jerk." In other words, a lot of people are not going to like you. It's really not people's business to figure out what's wrong with you. You know that you're wounded, but the sad thing is that you don't do anything about it. There is help available if you would just appropriate that help. The Holy Spirit is there to help you, too, but you've got to want His help.

Recover. For God's sake and your sake, don't allow anyone to run you down. Never be a trophy on anyone's shelf that says, "They just fell apart when I left them...." Help yourself. Get yourself together! Now, when people see you, they will see that they made the greatest mistake in their life by leaving you. They ought to hear about you and the great things you're doing before they see you. Don't just allow yourself to sit around and fall apart. If you do that, you will become "unloving" and "undesirable." Don't be foolish! Get it together and keep it together. If you can't do it for yourself, do it for God. You have destiny and purpose waiting for you!

RECOVERY TEST #1
(Answer key in Appendix A)

1) WHAT ARE THE FIRST STAGES OF RECOVERY?

fear, anger, depression
shock, denial, numbness
understanding, acceptance, moving on

2) WHAT ARE THE SECOND STAGES OF RECOVERY?

fear, anger, depression
shock, denial, numbness
understanding, acceptance, moving on

3) HOW IS DEPRESSION BROUGHT ON?

suppressed anger
suppressed fear
grieving over a loved one
one, two, or all three of the above

4) WHAT ARE THE LAST STAGES OF RECOVERY

fear, anger, depression
shock, denial, numbness
understanding, acceptance, moving on

5) GOING INTO EMOTIONAL SHOCK AFTER A TRAUMATIC EVENT THE PERSON BECOMES NUMB. ONCE NUMBNESS SUBSIDES, EMOTIONS RETURN. THIS IS CALLED:

Hitting Rock Bottom
Chronic Shock Syndrome
Processing Your Anger

CIRCLE "T" FOR TRUE AND "F" FOR FALSE FOR THE FOLLOWING:

6)   T   F   A person with a character disorder assumes too much responsibility; They say they have a problem.

7)   T   F   A neurotic doesn't assume enough responsibility; they don't see themselves as having a problem.

8)   T   F   When anger is turned inward it causes depression.

9)   T   F   When anger is turned outward it causes unforgiveness

10)   T   F   Anger gets you in trouble, but pride keeps you there.

11)   T   F   Repression is anger turned inside.

12)   T   F   It is impossible to work anger out of you.

13)   T   F   Shame is when someone or something causes us disgrace.

14)   T   F   Loneliness is not an absence of direction, it is an absence of affection.

15)   T   F   Anger usually is the result of people's needs not getting met.

.

16)   T   F   "Hitting rock bottom" is a phrase used to describe repression.

17)   T   F   Unreconciled loneliness will eventually move a person to a season of depression.

CIRCLE THE CORRECT LETTER FOR THE FOLLOWING:

When your sensitivity is worn down, when a foundation for immoral behavior is instilled, and isolation occurs, this indicates the stages of:

fear, anger, depression
shock, denial, numbness
understanding, acceptance, moving on

19)   What Book of the Bible shows the ups and downs?

Ecclesiastes
Song of Solomon
Psalms

20) Most people who are hurt go through a time of complaining and feelings of self-pity, otherwise known as:

The Lying Syndrome
The Elijah Syndrome
The Eli Syndrome

21)   What are the two things that abort healing/deliverance in your life?

anger and unforgiveness
fear and unforgiveness
pride and unforgiveness

FILL IN THE BLANK:

22)   Another name for "tormentors" according to Matthew 18 is _____.

SHORT ANSWER:

23)   Explain what "psychosomatic" means.

Recognizing the Signs

Chapter Nine

Physical and Emotional Signs
of Wounded People

Don't allow the bad things you experience in life
get on the inside of you!

THE PHYSICAL SIGNS OF WOUNDED PEOPLE

The Lord showed me that a lot of people are aging prematurely as a result of a wound they received sometime in their lives. This premature aging is not happening because they've been hanging out in the streets or doing drugs. Often adults can observe this in individuals that are close to our own age with whom we may have grown up. We believe that they are basically healthy people; however, when you see them, a question arises in your mind, "What could possibly have happened to make them look so bad, so worn out, and so old?" That person, more often than not, has been wounded by the storms of life. As ministers of the Gospel, we have to be watchful for this at all times.

The eyes are the windows of the soul...and they tell everything, Particular attention must be paid to the eyes. As you begin to look at a person's eyes, you can discover what seasons they've been through.

Did you not know that when you stand or sit before professional interviewers, they are taught to observe and make decisions based on your ability to look them into their eyes? They are told that if an individual cannot look them in their eyes, then he or she lacks self-confidence and should not be hired. Avoiding eye contact demonstrates a sign of weakness.

I have observed that people who have slightly bulging eyes may have suffered some sort of shock that almost devastated them. I've seen this more in women than in men, because a woman's natural tendency is to be more in touch with her feelings. People who have been severely hurt will often have blotches in their eyes. The white part of their eyes, the cornea, is hardly ever clear. When you look to the right or left of the pupil, you will see dark spots in their eyes.

When a person cries extremely hard, they can literally burst blood vessels in their eyes, and the signs of this linger behind. I'm not talking about red spots; I'm not talking about spots resulting from when they might have gotten drunk or high; I'm talking about the dark spots in the eyes that indicate hurt. And, the number of blotches and the darkness in color of the blotches seem to reveal and correlate with the extent of trauma the individual has suffered. People who have been put down or rejected never seem to look me in the eye. When I talk to them, they look down, they look off, or they look away. They cannot look anyone squarely in the eyes, because the eyes (the windows of their soul) are revealing their inner pain.

THE MIND AND THE BODY ARE LINKED

It is amazing that when you cry tears of joy, the tears are always sweet. But when you cry tears of sorrow, the tears are salty and bitter. How does the mind know that? The brain, the mind, and the optic nerve are connected. God ties them all together and tells them what to produce. When you are at your healthiest, the body actually produces healthy enzymes and hormones that make your body healthy. Untended hurts, grief, pain, and sadness will break down your immune system and cause you to become vulnerable to disease.

Satan knows the operation of man and he knows how God has made us. He works what he knows to destroy and break us down. Most doctors will tell you that some diseases are already in your body. It's when your immune system breaks down that they take over.

THE EMOTIONAL SIGNS OF WOUNDED PEOPLE

In the Book of Proverbs 18:14, it says:

> *"The spirit of a man will sustain his infirmity;*
> *but a wounded spirit who can bear?"*

When people are melancholy, unhappy, cantankerous, and when they have an inability to trust, they may be exhibiting signs of woundedness. You can tell the things from which you have not been healed by the things you feel uncomfortable talking about. If you are able to freely talk about the things that have wounded you, it means that you have been healed from it. But, when you can't talk about those things, or you can't talk because of anger, these areas of your emotions have not been healed.

I've discovered that a person who is not healed from emotional wounds will have another set of circumstances to contend with when the same devil that messed them up in that area begins to speak to them again. The desired end of this tactic is to develop low self-esteem within you.

Chapter Ten

Burnout

Learn as you grow older ...
work smart, not hard!

Each one of us is a potential target for "burnout." Burnout is a depletion of energy and a feeling of being overwhelmed. It is a condition wherein you cannot keep up with your usual round of activities. Burnout, psychologists say, is a syndrome of emotional exhaustion, depersonalization (you start looking down and talking down at people) and a reduction in personal accomplishment that can occur among individuals that do people-work of some kind. People suffering from burnout will show feelings of bitterness, anger, and resentment because they feel they are not appreciated for their efforts.

There are several factors of burnout, and these are symptoms that you can observe in yourself. People who have burn-out:

Feel that they need to prove something to folks
Put a lot of pressure on themselves
Never allot enough time for rest
Don't allow time for outside activities
Have trouble sleeping

It has been stated that half of the parents in America are suffering from burnout. Most professional people go through burnout sometime in their careers. Even ministers suffer from this because people can burn you out. People can vex you, and people can pull on you. As much as you love people, and as gregarious as you are, people can wear you out.

Burnout usually exhibits itself in some feelings of physical and emotional exhaustion. Victims frequently cannot face the future and detach themselves from any interpersonal closeness. Sensing themselves to be drained emotionally, they also suffer spiritually.

Burnout is a feeling of diminishing accomplishments that leads to stronger feelings of personal inadequacy, which further reduces accomplishments. Thus, the cycle of burnout is established. Burnout is a major reason why American industries have a hard time maintaining gains in productivity today.

PARADOX OF BURNOUT

Most of the tragic burnout cases in America tend to be people that are the most dedicated, the most devoted, the most loyal, the most committed, the most responsible, and the most highly motivated, educated, enthusiastic, promising, and energetic. They always suffer burnout first. Why? Partially, because these people are idealistic and perfectionists. They don't know when to say, "No." They expect too much of themselves as well as others around them. They work hard at being above average and doing more than what is required. They attempt to maintain a "break-neck" lifestyle.

DIFFERENT FORMS OF BURNOUT

There are many different forms of burnout that a person can experience. Some of them are as follows:

Job Burnout

The end result of prolonged job-related personal stress.

Mental Burnout

Feelings of frustration accompanied by a sense of helplessness, hopelessness, or self-doubt, which may lead to depression. Difficulty concentrating or paying attention, decreased self-esteem, disenchantment, disorientation, or just plain confusion.

Physical Burnout

Backaches, neck aches, migraines, insomnia, high blood pressure, loss of appetite, ulcers, constant colds, digestive problems, allergies, heartaches, heart attacks, and strokes can be mostly related to some form of physical burnout.

Spiritual Burnout

Usually, a gradually increasing fear that God is powerless, and that they, themselves, are the only ones who have the power to help correct their situation. They refuse to rely on God's power. They become disillusioned or feel like giving up, believing that others, including God, have given up on them.

Most burned out people are driven. They keep on going and ignore warning signs. When you are burning out, or burned out, you are not a nice person to be around. You're extremely cantankerous. You snap at everybody, no one can live up to your expectations -- otherwise known as a state of "depersonalization."

HOW TO RECOVER FROM BURNOUT

First, recognize that you are burned out. Shakespeare said, "To thine own self be true." Most workaholics are usually always burned out. Workaholics are motivated by FEAR or GREED. When you are in a state of burnout, you have no more energy to do anything, and then you begin to feel guilty about resting. You will start feeling guilty about taking care of yourself and then you will get mad when someone else tries to tell you about yourself.

Second, we must do something about it. Care for yourself and cultivate a spiritual life. Develop outside interests; learn not to be so hard on yourself; allow yourself a time to occasionally fail; and forgive yourself when you do fail, or fall, or don't live up to your own expectations. Sometimes, we're legends in our own minds. Many of us are simply too hard on ourselves; we should be led, not driven. You drive cattle, but you lead sheep.

Chapter Eleven

Co-Dependency

Never build your life around anyone
but Jesus. It's okay to build a life
together with a special someone!

When you are a co-dependent person, you are a parasite to the person you love. Co-dependent people always ask of people to do what they can do for themselves. Most co-dependent people are extremely immature. So, guess what, brother? If you marry a woman like this, it looks like she really loves you, but she's going to be your daughter for the rest of your life. Sister, if you marry a man like this, he's going to be your son for the rest of your life. You've got a boy on your hands.

Co-dependent people act like they cannot do anything. They will frustrate you if you don't know what you are dealing with. It seems like love, but it's a mental illness. It could be a real big ego trip for a man. He will think, "She loves me; she can't do anything without me." Love is not love when it smothers. Love is not love when it controls. And, most co-dependent people are manipulative. In other words, they will do anything to get your attention and receive your affirmation. They will lie: "I'm sick. Can you come home?" And, it won't be anything serious at all.

Most co-dependent people are starved for the attention that their moms and dads never gave them. You may think because you are 20, 30, 40, 50, or 60 years old that you outgrew something. You haven't. If it's in the root, it will be in the fruit. As an adult, you'll still search for what you never got as a child. The only difference between men and boys is the price of their toys. A lot of brothers have to be fathers to their wives. A lot of promiscuous young girls are that way because they are starved for male affirmation and they are striking back at their daddies (not their mothers). They are starved to the point that they become whorish. They never get fulfilled and, on top of that, they develop guilt, condemnation, and low self-esteem. It's a spiraling effect that has you ending up with an albatross around your neck that will drown you in disparity and self-hatred.

Dependency is an inability to experience wholeness or to function adequately without the certainty that one is being actively cared for by another. One may be dependent, but not "in love." In some of the relationships you were involved in, you weren't really in love. You were just temporarily insane and someone took advantage of your kindness. When you require another individual for survival, or when you "need" somebody in order to live, that's also being a parasite to that person.

I know a lot of beautiful "love" phrases you can say to people, but I'll never tell a woman, "I can't live without you." My existence today proves that's a lie! You should never tell a person, "I want to build my life around you." Straighten people out when they start telling you that. Say, "No, you want to build your life WITH me." Your life should never be built around anyone but Jesus. When people say that they want to build their lives AROUND you, they will have very high expectations of you. You may not be able to fulfill the job requirement. Don't allow yourself to be "ragged on," and don't become a parasite yourself.

Two whole and healthy people who love each other will be quite capable of living without each other; but choosing to live with each other is the blessing.

It's nice to say that someone is "so in love with you" that they can't live without you. But, that person is actually in a state of co-dependency. Their mental condition is thinking that, "If I can't have you, no one else will." They can become obsessed, and their obsession stems from co-dependency. Dependency in adults is pathological. It is always a sick manifestation of mental illness or mental defect. Yes, all of us have desires to be babied and to be nurtured without effort on our part. We also need to be cared for by a person stronger than us, who has our interest truly at heart. Sure, all of us have a desire to be cared for, but there is a limit that marks the line between healthy relationships and mental disorders.

PASSIVE DEPENDENT PERSONALITY DISORDER

The Passive Dependent personality disorder is the most common mental disorder in America. People with this disorder are seeking so hard to be loved, that they have no energy left to love. They are like starving people, scrounging wherever they can for food (love) and have no food (love) of their own to give others. They suffer from an inner emptiness, a bottomless pit crying out to be filled, which can never be completely filled. They tolerate loneliness very poorly. Because of their lack of wholeness, they have no real sense of identity. They define themselves solely by their relationships and by their possessions. They have a possessive spirit. It doesn't matter upon whom they are dependent, as long as they have someone. Consequently, those relationships, though seemingly dramatic in their intensity, are really extremely shallow.

Dependent people concern themselves about what others can do for them to the exclusion of what they can do for themselves. You can be so dependent that you ask the person you are insanely in love with to do something that you can do for yourself, like, "Honey, will you drive me to the corner?" And you have a driver's license.. Or, "Honey, will you come in here and wash my neck?" You can wash your own neck.

These people are so engrossed with the other person that they don't want to do anything for themselves. They want the person that they are attracted to do everything for them.

Sometimes you'll find older people will go back to their childhood and behave like this. They can become extremely possessive, too.

The only way to be assured of being loved is to be a person worthy of love. You cannot be a person worthy of love when your primary goal in life is to passively be loved yourself. Are you having your spouse do things for you, when you can do things for yourself? Sometimes in relationships, people become this way.

In a husband and wife relationship, each has to train the other how to love him or her, because how you love someone is different from how you want to be loved. Now, don't complain about what you permit. Sometimes we can get this "slave" thing going on. "Feed me, love me, wash me, cook for me, drive me." And they will drive you CRAZY!!

Passive dependency has it's root in a lack of love. It usually develops as a direct result of your parents not fulfilling the need for affection, attention, and care during your childhood years. Now, you want to make up for that deficiency with someone else. Some people cling so tight with desperation that it leads them to be unloving and manipulative in behavior. Passive dependent people lack self-discipline. They are either unwilling or unable to delay gratification of their hunger for attention. Consequently, they are endlessly angry, constantly feeling let down by others who can never, in reality, fulfill all their needs or make them happy.

This kind of person seeks to receive rather than give. They prefer to cling to childish things rather than grow. They labor to trap and constrict, rather than liberate. Ultimately, this person leaves a string of broken relationships behind and never becomes fulfilled. They destroy people because no one can live up to their expectations – no one can live up to their daily itinerary of meeting their selfish needs.

Co-dependency is not of God. Love does not control. If you're in a controlling relationship, it's not love. It's domination. Sometimes, when we finally find something that's good, we become manipulative about trying to keep it – even to the point of controlling it. This is especially true when it comes to women that love their men. They might start "marking" them, by dressing them (in an effort to control them). You are making sure that other women know that this is your man because you are both dressed alike.

Chapter Twelve

Sadness

Negative meditation produces sadness,
and that negative meditation
is called "stinking thinking!"

Sadness can sometimes be identified in the lives of people. Sadness signals hurt and loss. It helps us to grieve and to let go. Yet, sadness is always the path to joy, because it signals a hurt that needs to be processed.

Another aspect of sadness is tenderness. When people are sad, there's something that they are very sensitive about, and you should be very cognizant of that.

When you cannot feel sad, you usually become very cold-hearted. That means that you are shutting down your emotions. Now you are dangerous. In Matthew 24:12, Jesus says, "In the last days, the love of many will wax cold." This is the description of the cold-blooded, cold-hearted generation in which we live. There are folks that will do anything to you without losing an ounce of sleep. We're in a society of crazy people. We're in a sin-sick, mentally-sick society. In certain cities, the mindsets of people are unreal.

RECOVERY TEST #2
(Answer key in Appendix A)

1) WHAT IS "BURNOUT"?

a depletion of energy and a feeling of being overwhelmed

a condition wherein you cannot keep up with your usual round of
activities a syndrome of emotional
exhaustion all of the above
none of the above

2) PEOPLE WHO HAVE "BURNOUT" ARE USUALLY:

people who feel they need to prove something to others
people who put a lot of pressure on themselves
people who don't allow time for outside activities
all of the above
none of the above

3) PEOPLE WHO ARE CO-DEPENDENT:

require another individual for sound survival
feel they "need" somebody to live
a only
b only
both a and b

4) PASSIVELY DEPENDENT PEOPLE:

tolerate loneliness very well
have a possessive spirit
have no real sense of identity
both a and b
both b and c

MULTIPLE CHOICE: SELECT THE APPROPRIATE LETTER IN THE BLANK ON THE LEFT

Job Burn-out; b) Mental Burn-out; c) Physical Burn-out; d) Spiritual Burn-out

5)_____ Results from feeling frustrated by a sense of helplessness, hopelessness or self-doubt which may lead to depression.

6)_____ Results in back aches, neck aches, migraines, insomnia, ulcers, constant colds, allergies, and heart problems.

7)_____ This type of burnout is where a person becomes disillusioned or, feels like giving up, believing that others, including God, has given up on them.

Job Burn-out; b) Mental Burn-out; c) Physical Burn-out; d) Spiritual Burn-out

8)_____ Difficulty concentrating or paying attention, decreased self-esteem, disenchantment, disorientation, or confusion..

9)_____ Prolonged hours, resulting in personal stress.

10)_____ Where people think they are the only ones who have the power to help correct their own situations

FILL IN THE BLANKS:

11)_____ is a major reason why American industries have a hard time achieving gains in productivity.

12)Workaholics are motivated by
_____ or
_____.

13) To you, everyone is wrong and you are the only one that is right. That is called_____.

14)_____is an inability to experience wholeness or to function adequately without the certainty that one is being actively cared for by another. In other words, being a parasite.

15)_____   _____
_____   _____is a disorder whereby people are seeking to be loved, but have no energy left to love.

CIRCLE "T" FOR TRUE AND "F" FOR FALSE FOR THE FOLLOWING:

16)   T   F "Depersonalization" is when you start looking down and talking down to people.

17)   T   F   People who experience "burnout" usually show feelings of bitterness, anger and resentment because they feel unappreciated for their efforts.

18)   T   F   The most tragic burnout cases tend to be people who are the least committed..

19)   T   F   In recovering from burnout, you must first recognize that you are burned out.

20)   T   F   People need to occasionally allow themselves a time to fail and forgive themselves when they do.

21)   T   F   Most people who are burned out are led, not driven.

22)   T   F   When someone says that they "can't live without you," that person is in a state of co-dependency.

23)   T   F   Dependent people concern themselves about what others can do for them to the exclusion of what they can do for themselves.

24)   T   F   Passive dependency has its root in a lack of parental love.

25)   T   F   Passive dependent people are endlessly angry, because they constantly feel let down by others who, in reality, can never fulfill all their needs or make them happy.

The Healing Process

Chapter Thirteen

The Healing Process

All healing begins with a
positive, progressive attitude!

There are built-in emotional, self-protective measures with which God has equipped us. When you have been wounded, you need to recover. God designed our minds to heal themselves, given enough time and providing we yield to the healing process. The body, the mind, and the emotions have an enormous store of wisdom and divine intelligence, programmed into them by God.

Remember this analogy: When you break your arm, the doctor puts it in a cast to immobilize it – to take it out of action for a while, because it has been hurt and needs to heal. When you have gone through emotional hurts and traumas, your heart takes a beating. Just like your arm, it has been broken. You need to seek wise counsel, get some help, and even receive deliverance. Your heart needs time and proper care in order to begin to repair.

When your arm gets broken, you experience pain. Once a break has been diagnosed, the doctor immediately puts it in a cast. There will be a season of being uncomfortable in which you will still have pain. Your pain will eventually go away, but you will still have some discomfort. While your arm is being healed, yet isn't completely healed, it will begin itching; but it is still not ready to return to normal use. Guess what? The same happens with a broken heart.

A lot of you have rocky marriages because you didn't get healed from your last relationship. You ought not to begin a new relationship until you know that you are healed from the last one. But, you say, "Apostle, I've been divorced, I've been on my own, and I've been celibate for the last ten years." That doesn't mean anything, especially if you didn't get healed. You've just been ten years without someone.

If you go into another emotional relationship before you have been healed, you are headed for disaster. You are not strong enough emotionally to enter and succeed in that relationship. When a woman is pregnant, the baby draws energy and nutrients from every area of her body. This is also what happens in emotional relationships. People are pulling on you. Sometimes, the person you are in a relationship with doesn't understand that you don't have the strength to give them what they need. They'll start putting demands on you for things that your emotions are not steady enough to provide.

I see a lot of people going in and out of relationships in the first stage of recovery. You are very dangerous. First, you have to get healed so you can appreciate people again, or the devil will have you looking over your shoulder. He will have you really paranoid: "Uh-oh. This is the same thing the other person tried to do to me." You'll find yourself trying to be Sherlock Holmes. The devil will start talking to you, and he will even make sense about some things. He'll say, "Look how he did this and look how she did that. Isn't that what so-and-so said? Isn't that what so-and-so did?

Can you say you're in love right now? Whether your response is yes or no, don't ever forget this. What I tell you will let you know whether or not you are really in love. When you can let down your natural boundaries that protect your emotions in the company of the person, then you are in love. If your boundaries are up, or if your barriers are up, you are not in love. When you're in love, all of that comes down and you become extremely vulnerable.

Imagine if I move as though I am about to hit you. Your neck flinches and your eyes blink. It's a natural reaction. God designed us to protect our eyes, to protect our bodies when anticipating pain. When you see people in relationships flinching out of an instinctive need to protect themselves, know this: they haven't healed. If you notice this reaction in an intended spouse, you have to say, "Baby, let me let you go until you are healed. Now, have your psychologist give me a call...." That person is locked up in a season of hurt. Unless you possess tremendous wisdom and patience, that person is going to cause you a lot of problems.

There are a lot of people who have had broken hearts and they are not healed at all, yet they are trying to enter into another relationship. They must be itching for someone to find out that they emotionally do not have the strength to "give and receive" in a love relationship. People demand attention and affection, and when you don't have it to give, you don't have any business in a relationship.

Remembering the broken-arm analogy: the arm has begun to itch, you have now mentally moved into a season of anticipation. You can't wait. You believe your arm is okay. But, you must wait until the doctor does an x-ray to find out if it's totally healed. The doctor may remove the cast, and may put another one on. In the meantime, you think you're ready to use that arm. Just because it isn't bothering you anymore is not a sign that it's ready to be used. Your heart – your feelings -- are the exact same way. People often end up getting someone just like the one they left and get re-wounded. You need healing. When your heart has been broken, like the arm, it's time to pull back; it's time to draw back for a while, protecting and shielding yourself form any relationship. Clinical psychologists have said that if you have gone through a divorce, you don't need to be involved with anyone for at least two years! The trauma of being alone, the trauma of being rejected, the trauma of being "dissed," stripped, and embarrassed have had tremendous effects upon your mental psyche. It does not necessarily have to be divorce that you're recovering from; it can be a long-standing relationship in which you just knew that you were going to get married but didn't. If you haven't gotten through the shock yet, and then try to begin a new relationship, you may be hurt again.

Some people refuse to accept the injuries and, therefore, refuse to immobilize their wounded hearts. If you try to use your broken heart in new relationships, the results will be the same as when you try to use a broken arm – it will only cause you more pain. Proper healing requires that you understand your vulnerability and allow yourself the necessary time to heal.

I believe a lot of us transfer hurts from relationship to relationship. That's why some of us are angry. Psychologists call it projection. That's when you start expecting that person to do to you what that last person did to you. The devil will start giving you false evidence, but don't get caught up in that foolishness. There will be some similarities between them, because, whether you know this or not, most people are attracted to a certain kind of person. This does not mean that they will be the same. It's just what you are attracted to and you don't have to justify or be embarrassed by what you are attracted to.

LOOKING FOR FULFILLMENT

Human emotions don't like vacuums. They grope, become very desperate, as they attempt to find a place of refuge. Your emotions want so desperately to be loved, that if you're not careful, you will start compromising. This is why many women become whorish. They lay down with anything and anybody because they are so void emotionally. Needing to be loved, needing to be consoled, and needing to be held awakens the body to try to solve the problem. Your body will start to think, "Maybe if I do this, it will bring about fulfillment." It's not because you're a whore, it's because you are emotionally empty.

See, the devil had all of this planned. He was hoping to take you out with some AIDS or some venereal disease. All of these things were laid out in the scenario that the devil had planned for you. Not only for you to have gone through what you went through, but the devil says, "If I don't get you in the wash, I'll get you in the rinse." Because if the initial bomb that falls doesn't kill you, there's always the fall out; there's always the aftershock.

When people don't give their emotions time to heal, they can end up in two, three, and four divorces. There are some people that are so love-starved that they cannot tolerate a vacuum. They've got to have somebody – anybody. When people are like that, the devil sends all kinds of conditions their way. Any man that marries a woman that is emotionally starved ought to understand that she can go through men like you change underwear. It is better that you know this and be forewarned before you get involved with people for which you are not emotionally ready. A person can appear to be whole – they even look sane. But when you get involved with them, you will find out that they are "insane." You heard that old saying, "You can't judge a book by its cover." You can't see a person's emotional problems until they are really "out of the box." And what you see will let you know whether it's time to run. They may be all the way "out the box" somewhere in the twilight zone.

Psychologists say that most gregarious socialites are slightly schizophrenic, exhibiting multiple personalities. Very few people have seen the real person. The reason why they haven't allowed people to see them as they really are is because the person they are hiding has been hurt and their true self will continue to back up further and further until that person is almost non-existent. With most of us, the real person has not yet been seen.

Some of us are afraid to be ourselves because we've been hurt and we don't want that hurt person to be seen. It is very similar to sustaining a physical injury. If you have ever stubbed your toe, notice that you became very protective about that foot. If anyone looked like they were coming near your foot, you'd say, "Wait, wait, WAIT! What are you doing? That toe still hurts." And you start pulling your foot back. You become very defensive and protective of that physical member of your body. You didn't want anyone to even look at it. That's exactly what we do emotionally – we withdraw. The real you says, "You aren't seeing me." Then, what are we seeing? I don't know. Shaft, Mandingo,

Cleopatra Jones? Sometimes, driven by our insecurities, we try to be like other people; we try to talk like other people. We put up a facade. We observe this after we have been married to a person for a little while. The parts of him/herself that he/she have held back start to come out, and we reel from the shock of it.

Chapter Fourteen

Vulnerability and Trust

Never tell your problems to people
who cannot help solve them!

Some of us have grown up with the lie that says, "Be silent about what you're going through." But, it hurts too much to be quiet. You need help and you need it now. You may feel that you are betraying someone's trust, but when you need help, you'd better get some. Don't believe the devil's lie: "Be quiet. Don't think about it and it will go away."

You have to be vulnerable to get healed. You cannot be withdrawn, introverted, a recluse, a shut in, or a distant person and expect God to heal you. You've got to be vulnerable. When you submit yourself to the surgeon, you become anaesthetized. In other words, you submit yourself to the guidance and wisdom of the surgeon in order for your illness or injury to be treated. If you are seeking to be healed, you must become willing to endure the pain of statements that may bruise you, yet are a part of the recovery and healing process. You don't fight the surgeon, so don't fight the friend who loves you enough to tell you the painful truth. As Solomon said, "Faithful are the wounds of a friend" (Proverbs 27:6).

Every person in every condition must have an emotional

support base consisting of trusted, encouraging people. The people who depressed people associate with will be instrumental in extracting 50% of their pain, and their season of depression will be over sooner. In other words, a lot of the help you will be getting will be contingent upon the amount of people you submit yourself to for help. You need to empty out to someone.

If you don't have a trusted friend, ask God to send you one. "A brother," the Bible says, is raised up for adversity" (Proverbs 17:17). To get healed, you've got to make yourself vulnerable; you've got to open up to someone. That should be a person you can trust and to whom you can open your heart. Don't ever feel that you are "strong" by keeping quiet. Don't ever feel, brothers, that you are not a man because you want to share what's really bothering you. If you want to die, keep it to yourself. If you want to have a nervous breakdown, if you want to have a stroke, if you want to have a heart attack, keep it. But, if you want to live, if you want to be healthy, if you want to have peace of mind, and if you want God to heal you, sit down and talk about the hurts that have happened in your life. You have carried these things too long.

Anything you cannot talk about, you haven't been healed from. Satan delights in ignorance. He likes for people to think that they are "okay." And he loves quiet people. They are the first ones he kills. He loves quiet-natured people because they take a whole lot of abuse and don't talk to anyone about it.

It's bad to be crying on the inside. That's why God designed your tears to flow out so that people can see that you're hurting. Don't ever stop yourself from crying. Crying is a natural way for the body to cleanse itself and flush itself from hurt. Yet, society teaches our men that "You're not a man if you cry."

Jeremiah cried so much, they called him "the weeping prophet." You just need to cry. Get a good cry.

Sometimes we think we're being strong, but what we're being is stupid. If you get around these people with false strength, they'll tell you, "You're not supposed to cry. Wipe your face." If they were speaking truth, then why would the Bible say, "Weep with those who weep?" (Romans 12:15) Why would the Bible say, "Weeping may endure for the night, but joy comes in the morning" (Psalm 30:5). See, after you finish crying there's a new season coming forth. But first, we cry.

Never tell your problems to people who cannot help solve them. When you do that, you are only gossiping and you could be gossiping about yourself. Never share your problems with people who are incapable of helping you. This is foolish and stupid! Don't waste your time on people who don't want to be helped. How can you tell that they don't want any help...by their attitude. Your attitude reflects the willingness of your heart. Your arrogance always reflects your anger.

Solomon said in the Book of Proverbs (23:9), "Don't whisper wisdom in the ear of a fool." In other words, don't tell everyone your business. Share it with trusted people. It's a matter of you really wanting to "seek and find." All of us have been hurt in that we've shared things with the wrong people, but that doesn't mean that everybody is like that. Most of us are the "walking wounded" anyway.

Chapter Fifteen

Forgiveness

Whomever you do not forgive,
you become emotionally chained to!

It is imperative to know what forgiveness is and what forgiveness is not. It is important that you get a revelation of forgiveness and initiate it to enable you to progress pass denial. Forgiveness may be blocked by your own denial that you've been hurt.

Forgiveness comes from the heart. If it comes from the head, it's not real. God is very specific when He says that it must come from the heart. We say we forgive, but we don't act as if we have forgiven. Even if you don't feel like you've forgiven that person, act like it. Before long, your attitude will catch up with your actions.

Forgiveness does not mean that the other person was right and that you were wrong. Your sense of justice, coupled with an inaccurate view of forgiveness, can block your ability to get healed. But, I'll tell you what forgiveness is:

FORGIVENESS IS AN ACT OF YOUR WILL!

You love who you want to love; you hate who you want to hate; you forgive who you want to forgive. Never ask God to help you to forgive someone. It's an act of your will. For a Christian, it's even worse. Unforgiveness for a Christian means living a lie, because when you are born again, the very nature of God is in you. What is that nature? I John 4:8 says, "For God is love." The nature of God is love and the root of forgiveness is having love. You have no problem forgiving people you love, and you have no problem with forgiving people if you have God's love.

The Bible says, "While we were yet sinners, Christ died for (the ungodly)" (Romans 5:8). In other words, while you were hurting God, He still loved you enough to go to Calvary. And, you tell me you have that kind of love in you; the same love that Jesus had from Calvary when He said, "Father, forgive them for they know not what they do" (Luke 23:34)?

You tell me you have that same kind of love in you and you can't forgive? How many times were you whipped all night long? How many times were you speared in the side? Who drove nails through your wrists? Who drove nails through your feet? Who pulled all of the hairs out of your face? Who spat in your face as you carried a tree up a mountain? These are just a part of the persecutions our Savior suffered. The Bible doesn't tell us all of the persecutions Jesus went through, just the more vivid ones. You didn't go through that kind of persecution and pain. Jesus did, and He did it for you. "For He hath made Him to be sin for us, who knew no sin; that we might be made the righteousness of God in Him" (II Corinthians 5:21, emphasis added). He did it for you, but yet from Calvary, He could say, "Forgive them because they know not what they do." Can you say that? If you have the very nature of God in you, you can.

I can show you in the Bible where Stephen was being stoned to death in the Book of Acts. It says he looked up to Heaven and said, "Lord, lay not this sin to their charge" (Acts 7:60). That's the only time I find in the Bible where Jesus is standing on the right hand of the Father. Jesus got off the throne to see who was dying like Him. I'm sure He thought, "Who is this acting like Me? Of all the people on the planet, I finally have someone who talks like Me, who loves like Me. Who is this dying like Me!" I tell you, this is the only recorded Scripture in the Bible where Jesus is standing next to the right hand of the Father. He was there saluting His child!

God expects His children to forgive. Remember what John 3:16 says: "For God so loved the world that He GAVE His only begotten Son…" People who forgive have a lot of love. People who don't love can't forgive. God doesn't expect the world to forgive, because they don't have the capacity to forgive. But, He expects His children to forgive because we have His love. He forgave us when we were sinners, and now that He lives IN us, and lives THROUGH us, He wants us to act like Him.

I wonder how many times we get an opportunity to act like Jesus and don't. Peter said to Christ, "How many times must I forgive my brother?" (Matthew 18:21, paraphrased). Jesus said, "Seventy times seven" (v. 22). In other words, as often as your brother needs forgiveness, you forgive him. There is no number – who's counting? How many times do you breathe air? As often as you need it. How often must you forgive somebody? As often as they need it.

Once again, forgiveness doesn't mean that you agree with what they did. But, when you don't forgive, you are "chained" to the person who you won't forgive, and you are chained to the sin that caused that unforgiveness. You are chained to that event and to its memory. But, when you forgive, you cut that ungodly umbilical cord. Anybody that has unforgiveness can rehearse the hurt, bringing the hurt from the past to the present, like it just happened.

Forgiveness does not mean the other person was right and you were wrong. Forgiveness does not mean that all the pain vanishes instantly; but as soon as you forgive, the healing process begins. You take a giant step in healing when you talk about your pain. The healing is sometimes in chunks, sometimes in chips. When you deal with it, it disintegrates. Healing is an ongoing process.

The Bible says, "They shall lay hands on the sick and they shall recover" (Mark 16:18). Mental healing works the same way. Healing is an ongoing process and, while you're being healed, you need to avoid people and situations that may rewound you or have the potential to rewound you.

Forgiveness does not mean that you're letting the other person control you. It's just the opposite. Unforgiveness means the other person is controlling you. Forgiveness breaks that control. Whoever angers you controls you, even if they are deceased. Did you not know that some historians say that there are men who still rule from the grave...men like Sigmund Freud, Karl Marx, and Albert Einstein? It would be a travesty if a person that you haven't seen in years were still controlling you. That person could go on the ultimate ego trip: "I left them, but they still haven't gotten over me."

Refusing to forgive is like a wound that is gouged opened every day. Each day the wound gets worse because you keep reopening it through unforgiveness. Eventually, the wound gets infected. The pain of the wound grows and intensifies. This is what it is like when you do not forgive. Bitterness sets in and you keep hurting, even when the event that caused the pain is no longer happening. The person who you have not forgiven is still controlling you.

Forgiveness, by contrast, is like a wound that once was very deep but has been allowed to heal. This wound, as opposed to that of unforgiveness, has been treated. Now, it's just a scar. Each day you think less and less about the scar. You can look back at it, and remember something that was once very painful, but all you can see is a scar that continues to get smaller in size. You know the wound itself is just a memory. This is forgiveness.

Forgiveness is not just forgetting. Forgiving is more than forgetting. When someone says, "just forget it," that's foolish. Forgetting something cannot be done at will. We forget certain things when they are pushed out of our conscious thoughts, by thoughts that are more important to us. We forget things we seldom think about. Forgiving means moving on to focus on other things in a way that will cause the traumatic event from entering into one's conscious thoughts. So, forgiveness is not just forgetting; it's a conscious effort to move on to better things.

Forgiving someone doesn't mean that you are stupid. It simply means that you are willing to reconcile an offense even if the other person doesn't want to. Get it off of you, because you don't want your prayers hindered.

People who love a lot can forgive. People who can't love do not forgive. People who have little love can only forgive a little. I cannot convey to you how important it is for you if you have this problem. Deal with it immediately. It's equally important for me to convey to you, brothers and sisters, that you understand for whom and about what you are praying because you can be praying for people to get healed and those people refuse to forgive. Praying for them then becomes an exercise in futility. It won't work, I promise you. And the Scriptures explain why:

"Therefore is the kingdom of heaven likened unto a certain king, which would take account of his servants. And when he had begun to reckon, one was brought unto him, which owed him ten thousand talents. But forasmuch as he had not to pay, his lord commanded him to be sold, and his wife, and children, and all that he had, and payment to be made. The servant therefore fell down, and worshipped him, saying, Lord, have patience with me, and I will pay thee all. Then the Lord of that servant was moved with compassion, and loosed him, and forgave him the debt."

"But the same servant went out, and found one of his fellow servants, which owed him an hundred pence: and he laid hands on him, and took him by the throat, saying, Pay me that thou owest. And his fellow servant fell down at his feet, and besought him, saying, Have patience with me, and I will pay thee all. And he would not: but went and cast him into prison, till he should pay the debt. So when his fellow servants saw what was done, they were very sorry, and came and told unto their lord all that was done."

"Then his lord, after that he had called him, said unto

him, O thou wicked servant, I forgave thee all that debt, because thou desiredst me"
(Note: The Lord calls people who do not forgive WICKED.)

"Shouldest not thou also have had compassion on thy fellow servant, even as I had pity on thee?"
(Note: It takes compassion to forgive people.)

"And his lord was wroth, and delivered him to the tormentors, till he should pay all that was due unto him."
(Note: His lord was angry and delivered him to the tormentors (demons).

"So likewise shall my heavenly Father do also unto you, if ye from your hearts forgive not every one his brother their trespasses."

Matthew 18:23-35

Again, forgiveness is not just forgetting. Even though you may push past pains back into your subconscious, you must first confront and deal with the pain. If you are unwilling to confront the pain of your childhood years, your teen years, your adolescent years, or your adult years, you are in danger of engaging in a superficial forgiveness; a pseudo-forgiveness of people who really hurt you.

And, don't just say, "Oh, nothing's there." The Bible says, "The heart is deceitful..." (Jeremiah 17:9). Some people will lie. Some people I know were harboring unforgiveness but denied it. I had to ask the Holy Spirit to show them. He did. You can go through the whole day thinking that you lived so good for God, and right before you go to bed, the Holy Spirit will show you what you did or said to somebody to offend them. It takes the Holy Spirit, because God says, "My ways are not your ways, and like the heavens, my thoughts are higher than your thoughts" (Isaiah 55:8-9, paraphrased). You've got to do this kind of inventory or self-analysis and self-cleansing daily. Don't go to bed without cleansing yourself with the Blood of Jesus. Get that sin covered. "Be tenderhearted," Ephesians 4:32 says. In other words, be quick to forgive people. Even if you don't totally forgive them, act forgiving and your emotions will catch up with your actions. This is called maturity. But, when you are immature, you pout saying, "I'm just not going to forgive them and they will know that I'm not going to forgive them."

Watch people who have no problem with forgiving others. These are people who really love. Also, watch people who say, "I just can't forgive." They are not very loving. You don't need them around you because, being human, you are going to do something that offends somebody sooner or later. When you offend someone, you want to be able to go to him or her and say, "Will you forgive me. I'm sorry," and receive forgiveness.

As a man of God, as a teacher of this Gospel, and as an Apostle, I find unforgiveness to be 75% of the reason why people don't get healed. And then they will say, "That healing stuff doesn't work. I went up there and let them anoint me with oil. They prayed that prayer and I still didn't get healed." Now you know why. Change your attitude and God will change your altitude.

OFFENSES WILL COME

The Bible says, "...Offenses will come..." (Luke 17:1). It's impossible to live in a world without being offended. With some people, it's impossible to live one minute without being offended because you're just that touchy and fussy.

There is a certain personality trait that is very fussy, very irritable, and very mean. But, these people are usually very smart. They are intellectual, but they are very grumpy. That's why marriage is important. People need to be married so God can bring balance into their life, through their spouse. But, if you're not ready to repent of being mean and grumpy, you're not ready to be married either.

Don't try to get revenge from an offense. Let God take care of that, because God knows how and where to hit your offender. God knows where to get them where it hurts. Just because you don't see revenge take place today, or tomorrow, or next week, does not mean anything. "The eyes of the Lord are in every place beholding the evil and the good" (Proverbs 15:3). As one goes to God because of an offense, even regarding unsaved people, God's vengeance still works.

Some offenses can be so deep that you will have to say, "By faith, Father, I release this to You because just the thought of this devastates me." You've got to ask God to help you: "Help me, Father. I want to be more like You."

I really want you to understand that forgiveness is truly an act of your will. Furthermore, when we forgive, we relieve a great deal of mental and emotional stress that could have been used for nursing grudges. People who still have grudges and chips on their shoulders have not forgiven folks.

When you forgive, you don't have the energy to either nurse or rehearse hurts. You don't have the energy to be "knit picking," with your lip stuck out. When you forgive, a whole healing process comes to your emotional being. But, when we want revenge, when we want to retaliate, the whole healing process is delayed once again.

VENGEANCE IS MINE SAITH THE LORD

Heretofore, I've dealt with revenge mainly from a secular perspective; now, I will express this from a Biblical perspective: God says, "Vengeance is mine..." (Romans 12:19). Nobody gets away with anything. But, God is not angry with people like you think He is. When we get mad at someone, we think God is just as mad at them as we are. But, He's not, simply because God understands the totality of every person. We don't. We don't even understand ourselves like we should.

If God knows that someone has forthrightly, premeditatedly, and wickedly gone out to hurt you, God will avenge the wrong. But, it is our job as Christians to come to God and say, "Father, I've been wronged, I've been offended, I've been slighted, manipulated, exploited, or whatever. But, Father, I forgive him/her/them, and I release this matter to You." Amen.

Don't think this just works in the Kingdom of God. When two unsaved people are mistreating one another, it still works. The things that you do to someone when you are unsaved catches up with you in another relationship.

Do you know how God takes revenge for His children? He promotes you over your enemies. Would you rather God kill your enemies and you never see them anymore? Or, would you like for God to make you so rich that your enemies work for you. (People can repent.) This is how God gets revenge. I've seen this. He'll promote His children. As Joseph would say, "What the devil meant for evil, God meant it for good" (Genesis 50:20, paraphrased). God promoted Joseph over his brothers. They all had to come and bow down to him. He said, "I will make your enemies your footstool" (Matthew 22:44, paraphrased). God will do this if you give the matter to Him.

God tests your love sometimes by allowing you to go through an offense to see how you handle it. God wants to see if you are going to act like Him. Pressure reveals what is on the inside of you. When you squeeze a grape, whatever is in the grape will come out. God will allow you to be in a "winepress." When you get squeezed through pressure, what comes out of you?

GOD APPLAUDS FORGIVENESS

Stephen – this man's testimony of forgiveness made Jesus get up off of the throne. I repeat this to help you understand the extent of the importance of forgiveness in God's eyes.

We don't have the capacity to forgive in and of ourselves, but I John 4:8 says, "For God is love." When you have that kind of love, you have that kind of forgiveness. That is one of the untold mysteries of God – the manifold wisdom of God. His power is only matched by His love. That's awesome!

Chapter Sixteen

The Importance of Relationship

*You cannot grow using yourself
for a role model!*

Let me set something straight and don't ever forget it as long as you live. Genesis 2:18 said, "And the Lord God said, it is not good for man to be alone. I will make an help meet for him."

And earlier in Genesis we read:
"And God said, let us make man in our image, after our likeness; and let them have dominion over the fish of the sea, and over the fowl of the air, and over the cattle, and over all the earth, and over every creeping thing that creepeth upon the earth. So God created man in His own image, in the image of God created He him; male and female created He them." Genesis 1:26-27

The Godhead is a Trinity: Father, Son, and Holy Spirit. All three wrapped up into One Being. These three Persons are bound together in relationship. They are constantly communing and communicating. God is a God of fellowship, and He is a God of relationship. We have been created in His image and likeness so, therefore, we have the same needs and desires. God wants fellowship and God wants relationship.

God created man for Himself.

God is a social God. And when He created man, He said, "I want some more sons, I want some more daughters, and I want them to relate just like the Father, Son, and the Holy Ghost to one another. I want My children to be in relationship." Once we understand the social aspect of God and man, we can destroy the lie that has been spoken many times to people that have been hurt – "All you need is God." Every Christian has heard this before. It is just not true. That's just like saying, "All you need is to drink water everyday, and don't worry about food." You need to drink water, but eventually you're going to die if all you do is drink water.

God is our most important need, but what is also true is that you need me and I need you. God gave Adam everything he needed to fulfill his calling and purpose on earth. Man was a complete and perfect work, fashioned by the Perfect, All-Wise God and, yet, He beheld Adam and said, "It is not good for man to be alone." God formed man's spiritual being wherein He meets and fulfills our needs, but that is not all that we are – that is not enough.

The bad advice that you may have been giving people – "All you need is God – has got to stop being spread. Be true to yourself and be honest in witnessing. We are social beings. We need one another and we need people. The more anointed you are, you're going to see that you like people. I don't know if you realize it or not, but ministry is a people business and John Q. Public is a "trip!" You'd better be anointed or else you're not going to be able to handle it!

There is a part of you that needs God; and there is a part

of you that needs the company of a physical person. If you don't need physical people around you, you have developed a character disorder. Why don't more people live in rural areas...because there are not enough people. But, if you are an urban person, you like seeing people. You don't like putting that much distance between you and another person. You'll say, "My God, the next house is 50 miles down the road! I don't mind being separated from some folks, but I want to see people. I don't just want to see cows, ducks, or buffalo." God knew that the man needed someone he could touch, someone he could talk with, someone he could laugh with, and someone he could make love with. That's the first thing Adam did when he met his wife. The Bible says that Adam knew his wife; that is, he had a sexual relationship with her.

SEX

Do you know that when you are in love, you are sexually attracted to the person? I didn't say you were acting like a whore or a whoremonger; I said you were sexually attracted to the person. We fall in love and we are either conscious or unconscious of being sexually attracted to somebody. Sex and love have an erotic link. That's why you must be careful, because when you are in love with someone, you want to go to bed with him or her whether or not you're going to admit it. Oh, I know, you're so holy that you don't want to admit it, but it's true anyhow!

Let me say this to the brothers: if you think you are going to be so saved that your sex drive will go away, you're fooling yourself! This is the problem. This is what we've done as Christians. We've said, "After you get saved, everything else is going to die." Are you in for the greatest shock of your life! You are dying to self; and when a dying to self takes place, you come alive in Christ. If anything, your sex drive ought to be more under control, but to say it won't be there anymore would be fooling yourself! Your sex drive will be there because God designed it to be there. He just wants it under control.

Chapter Seventeen

The Ministry

When you give God a life,
surrendered and committed,
God can then give you a ministry.

Many of God's ministers are hurt today, because they have
been so busy ministering to others, while in need of being
ministered to. You've been so busy raising the dead, casting
out devils, and laying hands on the sick until you become ill
yourself.

You'd better make sure that when you are praying for
people that you have an anointing on you. If you are praying
for people without an anointing, you can pick up their
demonic spirits. This is what is referred to as "transferring of
spirits." If you are just jumping up to impress people so that
they can see you praying for people, those spirits can transfer
onto you. Don't do that. If you are praying for people and
you're not under a spiritual covering (not affiliated with a
local church), you will put yourself in a dangerous position.
Demons are legalists, and they know the conditions under
which they can operate. If you get "out of bounds" with God,
you are fair game. Get a copy of the book Spiritual
Authority, by Watchman Nee, and you will understand how
you need to operate within the boundaries of God's Word as
well as the authorities that He has put over your life.

Authorities are in your life because God is a God of order, and He expects you to do things "decently and in order."

I learned a long time ago, if a person that I'm praying for doesn't get healed, that's not my problem. When I first started praying for people, the devil said, "Look, nobody is on the floor." You'll find that when some preachers pray for you, they will throw you on the floor. Your neck will be pulled back so far that you will look like a "Pez container." I watch a lot of preachers, and they think that the only thing that validates their anointing is multitudes of people sprawled on the floor. God is in the process of picking people up, not knocking them down. I don't care if nobody hits the floor – especially if you're real big – I don't want to pick you up! I could slip a disc in my back!

When I go to pray for people, I quickly ask the Holy Spirit to show me the attitude of those for which I am praying. Sometimes when I'm praying for folks, I will walk right past somebody because I have an anointing on me. I will not waste it on you if you've got an attitude. It all starts with your attitude. Quit being mad at folks, and let go of your anger. Are you going to get mad at the puppet or are you going to get the puppeteer? That person that dissed you is nothing but a puppet, so get that puppeteer and cut those strings! Be smarter than the devil. We're not ignorant of Satan's devices. He works in patterns. You can see his stuff coming. "A wise man sees the danger and hides himself, but a fool continues on and is punished" (Proverbs 22:3, paraphrased).

Some people have bad attitudes about their pastors. Don't counsel with people who have not gone to their pastors first. I've asked people if their pastors have released them to talk to me, and they have told me "no." I tell them to go and get a release. If they tell me they don't want to tell their pastor, then I inform them that they don't want to tell me either. If they say something like, "Well, my pastor doesn't understand," then I want to know why they are still there.

Sometimes people have a very unappreciative attitude. I used to cast demons out of folk night and day, but when the time came to receive an offering for support of my ministry, these people were nowhere to be found. I'm good enough to cast devils out of you, but I'm not good enough for them to support me financially. So, I started asking them where they were sending their tithes. Wherever they would tell me, I'd tell them, "Well, maybe, that's where you need to go for prayer and counseling." (If I'm going to wreck the car, I'm going to drive it!) You are going to have to be selective and scrupulous while dealing with folks.

HEALING AND DELIVERANCE

When you minister effectively to "sick" people, it is not hard to perceive their state of being. A spirit of infirmity means a demon of disease. It is not always the laying on of hands that people need, because healing sometimes means deliverance, and sometimes deliverance means healing. The Gadarene demonic needed to be healed. But it was a different kind of healing that he needed. Deliverance sometimes blocks healing, and sometimes deliverance is healing.

God instructed me: "Tell them when they pray for people to be delivered from something, ask the Spirit of God to heal the area where the enemy has occupied." If the devil is lurking in a certain area of one's body, whether it be in their mind, their back, their stomach, or wherever damage was done. You will have to ask God in prayer to reveal where the enemy has occupied and ask, in Jesus' Name, for a healing balm to be ministered in that area. Pray for the area that is wounded. It must be healed and it will heal; but you have to "dress the wound" so that it will heal properly. If you had wild horses in your living room, what would you expect your living room to look like? The horses did some damage. Well, if a wild animal does damage, what do you expect the devil to do? This is his ministry…to do damage and wreck your house.

Jesus said to me a few years back, "The devil always leaves trying to tear up something before he leaves. He will not leave peacefully. Before he leaves, he's going to do some damage. Before you cast him out, he's going to do some damage." The Holy Spirit will leave as peacefully as He came. The Bible talks about how spirits tear people…making them fall down on the ground and look like they're having seizures. And some of them are having seizures. "Tear" means to cause some physical eruption or damage in the body before he comes out. Some epileptic seizures are demonically inspired.

IT MIGHT BE JUDGMENT

There are some people upon whom God has placed His hand. If God is whipping them, there's not a prayer that you can pray to stop it. Paul said in Hebrews (10:31), "It's a fearful thing to fall into the hands of the Living God." I don't care how much intellect you have or how many psychoanalyses you've made in your own little professional, scrutinizing, analytical brain; God can allow some new pain to come on you that you've never heard of before. Doctors say that there are over 800 new diseases that are discovered each year. They don't even have names for them. They just give them numbers: "This is the XK47 disease."

Many of the healings that people get are conditional. Whatever God healed you from is going to show up again, if you don't meet the conditions. Satan (after he gets his butt whipped) will leave folks for a season. But, when he shows up, folks will call on you to lay hands on them again.

Disobedience gives Satan a legal right to attack you. And God will not do anything about your attack until you get into a place of repentance. You see, you can't play with God. You may play with your husband or your wife, and kids may play with their parents; you may try to get over on your boss, and fool your pastor; but God is not going to play with you!

Chapter Eighteen

Getting in Touch with Your Feelings

*You cannot heal
what you cannot feel!*

Feelings always demand expression. Feelings that are held inside will find a way out. Feelings express themselves in unplanned ways when denied. Illnesses can result sometimes from internalized feelings. Do you have a lifetime experience of blocking or delaying your feelings? It will take time to learn to identify the feelings you have been shutting off. Some of us have ignored our feelings for so long, we don't even know who we really are.

Men and women do not express their feelings the same. A man is going to tell you what he is thinking, but a woman is going to tell you what she is feeling. A woman is usually in touch with her feelings. She can be very emotional during certain seasons. She must be careful, because her emotions can get her in trouble. A woman may think she is hearing from God, but it is her emotions leading her.

Consider this as a word of advice if you are entering into a relationship. See how even-tempered a person is. I don't think it would be wise to get into a relationship with someone who is not in touch with his or her feelings because it may mean that they are avoiding something. They might be running or hiding from something. Usually people who are in touch with their feelings verbalize it. They're also melodramatic: they talk with their hands. They're "touchers"; they're feelers. When they talk, they've got to grab your hands; they've got to touch you or squeeze you.

Some people are more in touch with their feelings than others, and they readily express their feelings. Others are introverted. In other words, they feel that if you are going to talk to them, you've got to come into their sphere. Everyone has an imaginary sphere around him or her. If an introvert shakes someone's hand, you will notice him or her stretching their arm, keeping you at a distance, and out of their imaginary sphere, out of their personal space.

EXPRESSING OUR FEELINGS

Sometimes instead of expressing your feelings, you may run away from them. You should learn to identify the techniques you use to run away from your feelings. You should try to get in touch with your feelings.

You may have learned to live on someone else's feelings rather than your own. Your family may have discouraged you about displaying your feelings by saying things like, "You'd better not cry." Or, "Why are you smiling? Why are you grinning like an old Cheshire cat?" These are techniques your mom or dad taught you because they themselves may have been introverted. The truth of the matter is that your mom or dad may have really been "crazy." You may have been with parents who failed to raise their children properly. Now, the children are misfits as adults because they want to be themselves, but were taught, for a long time, not to be.

Some parents don't like to see you smile, and some parents don't like to see you laugh too much. Some parents just don't like laughter. One thing my parents didn't like when I was growing up was "signifying," that is, talking about each other. When I was growing up, "black" was a bad word. When somebody called you "black," it was time to fight. "Who's Black?" "Black" was a fighting word!

You may have been taught that certain feelings were acceptable and certain feelings were not acceptable in your house. Now, as an adult, you've got to learn how to be in touch with your feelings and how to express them. Because we've been hurt, we feel that expressing our feelings makes us vulnerable. Husbands and wives especially think that expressing themselves makes them vulnerable. This may sound crazy, but I know what I'm talking about. You can be married to someone that's afraid to express their love to you. You may wonder how can this be? But, because they've shut that area down for so long, they don't know how to jump-start it. When you leave the cables off of the battery in your car for a long period of time, and then hook-up those cables again, see what kind of battery you've got. Your feelings are the exact same way. Disconnect them and hook them up again to see if you can get them to start. Do you need a jump-start?

TECHNIQUES IN AVOIDING FEELINGS

There are techniques in human behavior people use who have some behavior problems. They use these techniques to avoid their feelings.

1) Intellectualizing

This means that you try to keep your thoughts and conversations on rational things when you feel a flood of emotion coming on. When that flood of emotion comes, you begin talking about intellectual matters rather than your feelings. You talk until you do not feel the emotion any more. There is nothing wrong with being intellectual, but there is a time to be intellectual. When you and your husband are making love, it's certainly not time to talk about intellectual things like Einstein's Theory.

2) Minimizing

This is similar to denial. When a person is minimizing, they are downplaying their pain experience or a bad experience. A woman may have been in an abusive situation with a man who was beating her in the head. Her response is, "At least he didn't kill me." When all it would have taken was one more blow to the head before he did kill her. Or, a man may say, "My last girlfriend took all of my money, but she left me bus fare to go to work." These are examples of downplaying your experiences.

3) Isolating

This is retreating into your own private world where you can control your feelings. You create an imaginary world. In other words, you are present physically, but you are thousands of miles away emotionally. I see a lot of this happening among people, who are relatively peaceful-natured, calm, and quiet. This happens to all of us periodically, especially when we get bored, and this can happen in a relationship. It can happen before a relationship, which may never come into existence because you are so busy retreating.

Isolating is a form of escapism. You could be in a bad relationship with a person and start fantasizing about another person you wish you were with. Whether you know this or not, you could be creating a bad habit that could be potentially dangerous to relationships. You can be with a person who loves you, but you are still wandering. Have you ever been with someone but it seemed like they weren't with you? You have to try hard to get their attention: "Hey, hey, earth to Ken...." Sometimes people can be so hurt, that they literally do this; or they do this because they are bored.

When you see people "tripping" like this, it's called isolating. It's dangerous because it can lead to some serious withdrawal in a person, and they may ultimately go into a shell.

4) Shyness

Extreme shyness is a mental disorder. Most people who are shy have it. They feel like they don't have anything to say. They may feel like the reason they don't want to talk is because they fear saying the wrong thing or they don't want to be seen. They really don't want any attention. With that kind of attitude, how can you witness for God? The Bible says that the saints are "as bold as lions" (Proverbs 28:1). How can shy people go out and tell others about Jesus? I know some of us have personalities that are more bold than others. Some of us are naturally extroverted. I'm extroverted. I'll talk to a rock. I don't have any problems talking to anyone; I can get along with anybody. I learn how to adjust to people. I need people, yet there are times when I don't need to be around anyone. But, I like people. I'm very gregarious; I like to entertain people, and I like to be entertained.

God designed us as social beings. God Himself designed us the way He is because He is a sociable God. He designed us to relate the same way that the Father, Son, and Holy Ghost relate, who continually commune with each other. When you say you don't need people, or you don't ever want to be around anyone, then you have a social disorder. You need to deal with that. I know that sometimes people can wound you and make you want to run away, but you ought to get over some things sometimes.

5) Swallowing the Feeling

When you are on the verge of being angry or upset, you sigh deeply, you take a deep breath, you swallow with a gulp, you engage in some type of physical activity, and that holds back that feeling. Some people actually have the problem of "swallowing their feelings." It's a problem because, once again, feelings should be expressed. You may not have this problem, but there are others who do; and these are emotional mishaps that we have to overcome. But, any habit learned can be unlearned. Many of us don't break habits because we don't replace a habit with a habit. If you don't replace a habit with a habit, there's a void. That vacuum needs to be filled.

6) Taking Care of Others

When in this syndrome, your focus is on someone else rather than yourself. You are eager to help someone else solve their problem, but you really don't want to solve your own. Have you ever talked to people like that? They want to know, "How are you doing?" When asked how they are doing they say, "Oh, don't worry about me." They don't ever want to share how they are doing. Now, there is a difference when the person wanting to share is a gossip. Now, I'm going to tell it to you straight; don't tell all of your business to anyone. Anyone who tells all of his or her business is a fool.

7) Uttering Your Whole Mind

The Bible says, "A food uttereth his whole mind" (Proverbs 29:11). If they are going to tell you all of their business, they will have no problem telling other folks all of your business. Be careful of people who want to know all of your business. There should be very few people in life who you allow to get that close to you, simply because one doesn't get very many true friends in life. There is a big difference between a friend and a fiend.

To the ladies, I need to tell you that some of you talk too much. I don't mean to be sexist, but you tell too many people your business. It is not wise to get other people involved in your business. "Too many cooks spoil the broth" and it wastes your time.

RECOVERY TEST #3
(Answer key in Appendix A)

1) FORGIVENESS MAY BE BLOCKED BY YOUR OWN_____THAT YOU'VE BEEN HURT.

anger
acceptance
denial

2) PRAYING FOR PEOPLE TO GET HEALED WHO REFUSE TO _____ IS AN EXERCISE IN FUTILITY.
move on
forgive
speak in tongues

3) YOUR _____ REFLECTS THE WILLINGNESS OF YOUR HEART.

attitude
arrogance
anger

4) YOUR ANGER ALWAYS REFLECTS YOUR_____:

attitude
arrogance
anger

5) "DON'T LET THE SUN GO DOWN WHILE YOU ARE STILL ANGRY." WHERE IS THIS SCRIPTURE FOUND?

Ephesians 4:6
Ephesians 4:26
Ephesians 2:6

SHORT ANSWER

6) Why is the heart like a broken arm? Explain the analogy.

7) How does God like to get revenge for His children?

CIRCLE "T" FOR TRUE AND "F" FOR FALSE FOR THE FOLLOWING:

8)   T   F   Forgiveness is just forgetting.

9)   T   F   Forgetting something can be done at will.

10)   T   F   Forgiveness means that the other person was right and that you were wrong.

11)   T   F   Forgiveness is an act of your will.

12)   T   F   The root of forgiveness is having love.

13)   T   F   Forgiveness means that you agree with what they did.

14)   T   F   You are chained to the person whom you don't forgive. You are chained to that sin, offense, event, memory, etc.

15)   T   F   Forgiveness does not mean that all the pain vanishes instantly.

16)   T   F   Unforgiveness means that the other person is controlling you.

17)   T   F   Forgiveness is a wound that has been treated.

18)   T   F   It takes compassion to forgive people.

19)   T   F   Real forgiveness comes from the heart.

20)   T   F   Forgiving someone means that you are willing to reconcile an offense (even if the other person doesn't want to).

FILL IN THE BLANK

21) A man's going to tell you what he's _____, but a woman is going to tell you what she's_____ because she's directly in touch with her emotions.

FILL IN THE BLANKS WITH THE TECHNIQUES USED TO AVOID FEELINGS

22) _____ means that you try to keep your thoughts and conversations on rational things when you become emotional.

23) _____ is when a person is "down-playing" a bad experience (i.e., "He hit me in the head, but at least he didn't kill me).

24) _____ is when you retreat into your own private world as a form of escapism, going into a shell.

25) _____ is when you are on the verge of being upset, you sigh deeply, take deep breaths, and swallow with a gulp. You engage in physical activities that hold back feelings.

26) _____ is when you focus on someone else's problems rather than your own problems. You're eager to help solve someone else's problems but don't want to solve your own.

FILL IN THE BLANK

27) Like a grape, pressure reveals what is on the _____ of you.

Chapter Nineteen

The Need to Love Yourself

Rejection is the emotional "disease"
of feeling "not good enough"
about yourself.

If you don't love yourself enough, you will have low self-esteem. When you love yourself too much, you become narcissistic -- tremendously vain, for a better choice of words. So, you need to have a balance, and the Holy Spirit can bring that. Mark 12:28-31 says:

"One of the teachers of the law came and heard them debating. Noticing that Jesus had given them a good answer, He asked him, 'Of all the commands, which is the most important?' The most important one, answered Jesus, is this: Hear, O Israel, the Lord our God, the Lord is One. Love the Lord your God with all your heart and with all your soul and with all your mind and with all your strength. The second is this: Love your neighbor as yourself. There is no commandment greater than these."

Now, this may sound a little "corny" to you, but if you're not loving yourself, you're disobeying God's command -- you're in sin. Think about it: how can you love me when you don't even love you? It might be that some people need to learn how to love themselves, and then they will know how to appreciate others.

If a person can't take care of himself, how can he take care of someone else? If a person can't cook for themselves, how can they cook for another? If a person can't drive themselves, how can they drive someone else?

Sometimes, we become involved with people and really don't have the capacity to love them. Believe it or not, our expectations can be too high -- because if you have been wounded or if you've suffered some type of loss, I can guarantee that your expectations of a relationship are extremely high. In other words, you want to be pampered.

So, you're hurting and want to be pampered. What if you're involved with someone who has gone through just as much loss as you have? How can they reasonably measure up to your expectations.

There are three types of love: phileo (friendship), eros (attractive appeal), and agape (God's unconditional love). Most worldly folks know the "phileo" type of love. From this we get the world "Philadelphia." That's really not love at all because it's conditional. It says, "I'll love you, if you love me." The eros love from which we get the word "erotic" means "I'll love you in the bed." This is not love either. At best, it could be an expression of love. That's the love the world understands. It does not understand AGAPE or unconditional love.

Let me ask you something from a spiritual perspective -- how can you go to an unbeliever and expect them to love you when they don't have the capacity to love? For if God is love, how can you expect His nature to be manifested in a person who does not have God? This is one of the many reasons why God tells us not to have any fellowship with unbelievers; because a nonbeliever doesn't even have a revelation of love.

It's dangerous for us as Christians to have relationships with nonbelievers because they don't know where you're coming from. I Corinthians 2:14 says, "The natural man receiveth not the things of the Spirit of God for they are foolishness unto him." The Bible also says, "The preaching of the cross is foolishness unto them that perish" (I Corinthians 1:18, paraphrased). But, foolishly, there are people who are still attempting to make relationships with people who aren't saved. The Bible warns us in Proverbs 25:19 (paraphrased), "Having confidence in an unfit person is like eating with a broken tooth or walking with a foot out of joint." Uncomfortable, isn't it?

And, all of you sensitive people, do you know what I've discovered? If you are as sensitive as I am, you've probably learned this hard lesson that I learned: It's best to have a relationship with people who are as sensitive as you are. In other words, find a person who is even tempered. I'm talking about a person who has the capacity to love. Don't try to cultivate that in anybody. There are some things we ought to be honest about. Whenever you fall in love, you shouldn't have to hold his or her hand and tell them how to love you. Marriage and serious relationships are for men and women; little boys and little girls need not apply. You want someone with experience in how to love you. When I say experience, I'm not talking about...you know where I'm coming from!

Sisters, you want to be treated like a lady. You don't want a little boy who has to be told, "Will you please open the door for me?" or "Will you please pull out the chair for me?" or "Please don't belch in front of me!" or "Please don't clean your teeth at the dinner table!"

Chapter Twenty

Recovery

*You don't drown by falling
into the water ... but by staying in the water!*

Recovering from hurts and losses is a process and it takes time. When you resist your time to mourn, you interfere with your body's natural stage of recovery. Some of you are still in mourning over a loss. I don't care if it happened 40 years ago, if you never allowed yourself time to heal, you're still in mourning. How long will I have a toothache? As long as you have a rotten tooth and a nerve. If you have to fall in love with someone in the natural, why not let it first be yourself? Part of your recovery is learning to love yourself. Do you really love yourself?

When you're going through this healing process, it's important to keep decision-making down to a minimum. Expect your judgment to be clouded. Postpone all major decisions for a while. If possible, delegate, relegate, and rest. When you're going through an emotional season of loss, rejection, hurt, or some other form of pain, be kind to yourself. The bottom line is that you really don't love yourself. If you come out of a beating, you can continue the beating by abusing yourself.

Be gentle with yourself. Don't rush about. Your body needs the energy for necessary repair. Learn how to take time to think on the Word and meditate.

When you've gone through emotional hurts, it drains you emotionally and physically. Rest is the foundation of health. Sleep more. Arrange your life so that you have lots of rest. Schedule it into your day. Plan to go to bed a little earlier and sleep a little bit later. Too much change has already taken place in your life and that's why you're hurting. Don't take on new responsibilities. Avoid situations in which you may be stressed, challenged, or upset. Why? Because it exacerbates the problem. I know life doesn't like vacuums. Sometimes, when we're out of love with somebody, we feel as if we've got to hurry up to fill that void. But we know what that is -- we've already talked about co-dependency.

When you are going through something traumatic, accept the fact that it is debilitating and it will take a while before you are completely well. You don't always have to tell someone that you've gone through a "debilitating, traumatic, exhausting" experience. It's not anyone's business. You've got to start looking out for yourself. A lot of us have not gotten the help we need because we were waiting for someone else to do it for us. So, you may be just as co-dependent as anyone else. There's something wrong when you don't take care of yourself. We all know the idiom: "Self-preservation is the first law of nature." The Bible commands us to love ourselves. It's a commandment; but the Holy Spirit brings balance so you don't become narcissistic, vain, and all-around conceited. But, you need to love yourself.

You can enter into a relationship with a person who is starting to love themselves after having been through hurt.

You'd better put some distance between you and that person until he or she has gotten healed. Because, when you have been hurt, you need to back off from people and love yourself for a while and be "stingy" about yourself. Don't try to divide your energy in trying to make the other person happy, because you don't have the strength or the capacity to love them like they would want or like you should.

Allow yourself time to be healed. If you spend time loving on others, that's less time you will have to love yourself, which means you will stay in that season of hurt longer. Stay focused on YOU.

The biggest mistake you can make when coming out of a bad situation is trying to rekindle that old relationship. I believe if it's God, that person will be there, no matter how long he or she will have to wait for your healing. I believe this philosophy: Catch the flight. If that's your baggage, it will catch up with you. Understand this: we need to be kind to other people's feelings. You need to explain some things. (Of course, we're talking about single people.) You owe an explanation to that person. Anything that God has for you is worth waiting for. God knows what season you are in, so why would He send you something to retard your progress. Think about that. It's not like God to work against Himself.

Invest your energies in healing and learning how to let go. This is one of life's greatest lessons. I Thessalonians 5: 21b commands us to: "Hold fast to that which is good...." The flip-side of that is to let go of that which is bad. You can be in a season of denial saying to yourself, "It wasn't that bad." Some secular songs will mess you up and will have you holding on to a lie. Some of that music will bring back old desires. Your flesh likes to be stroked. You can become an addict to anything to which you yield your members.

You can have some serious withdrawal pains, withdrawing from love and sex, just like a person on dope. God wanted a husband and wife to be together and make love and be so dependent on each other in that area. Whether you know this or not, your body gets used to it. Your body becomes dependent on this. If you yield to your desires and keep opening up a door of infidelity, you will end up in bondage. Some of you have some serious sexual DT's. Many of you have compromised; not because the man or woman was so good looking, but because your body was aching for sex. Your body was going through some serious withdrawal pains. Remember, image creates desire. So, be careful what you focus on. Don't try to rekindle old relationships.

Co-dependent people have some of the most serious problems in relationships. One problem with co-dependent people is their "people-itis." They're addicted to relationships. They get out of one relationship and get right into another one. They get rid of someone and get somebody else, just like the last person they had. The new person will even look like the last person. So we see, a problem unlearned is a problem returned.

Instead of investing your energies in a relationship while you're being healed, invest your energies in yourself. I believe when you are going through a season like this, you ought to have a good friend (of the same sex). As you talk and submit yourself to them, tell them of the person you're thinking about getting involved with before you do. Remember, you're not thinking too clearly, so you might as well have someone you can talk to who will be rash with you and be there to help you. Keep in mind, Satan will send these pseudo-lovers into your life. He'll send people who act like they have your best interest in mind. Have a friend you can talk to, preferably a saved friend. The world will tell you, "You need a lover. How long has it been? You're going to go blind if you don't get a lover soon." They will even accuse you of being gay just because you don't want to be a whore or a whoremonger anymore. They will try setting you up with people.

Be careful when someone tells you they have a friend they want you to meet and how "nice" that friend is. What do you mean "nice?" Monkeys are nice. Blind dates will make you go blind! Give your body the rest it needs.

Daniel 7:25 cautions us that Satan will send demons to come and "wear out the saints of the most High God." The devil doesn't have to wear you out when you're already burned out. Because of bad information, or no information, saints are not taking care of themselves.

Most people that are psychotic usually have some chemical imbalance in their bodies. The brain releases many hormones that help to heal the body. When the body is going through trauma, certain parts of the brain shut down. Those hormones we need are not released. A CAT scan is where doctors take a picture of your brain to see if there are any abnormalities like lesions, tumors, etc.

Laughter is medicinal. It releases hormones that are good for the body. This is why the Bible resolves that "A merry heart doeth good like a medicine, but a broken spirit drieth the bones" (Proverbs 17:22). Be careful about being in seasons of unhappiness for any prolonged period of time. The devil can't make a man, but he can cause some things to happen to us emotionally, knowing that it will shut down some vital organs that secrete hormones that cause our bodies to function. When those hormones are not secreted, when that immune system is broken down because of stress, Satan walks in with diseases. You've got to start taking care of yourself. Stop looking for people to diagnose what is wrong with you. If you aren't feeling right, then you diagnose it. If you can't, then go to the doctor or a therapist, and get some help. Stop sitting there feeling sorry for yourself. People can't read your mind. Don't be over-spiritual and expect the Holy Ghost to tell someone your problem.

Some of the problems we experience aren't spiritual, but natural. Drinking water helps to flush out your body. When your body doesn't get enough water, it holds on to water, thinking that it's going to dehydrate. Water has healing properties in it. Simple water helps to heal the body. This is one of the reasons why it takes us longer to come out of many of our problems. Start eating more fresh fruits and vegetables. Reduce your intake of caffeine and eliminate all nicotine and alcohol. Get junk food out of your diet.

God has no problem with anything you eat in moderation. But, when, for example, you eat red meats every day for breakfast, lunch, and dinner, you are asking for trouble.

Take a good multi-vitamin supplement. There are excellent herbal nutritional supplements. When I was going through some things, I began taking an herbal nutritional supplement and it has made a big difference. People with people-related jobs need special energy to deal with people. Doctors say you need vitamin B, C, Calcium, and Potassium. Anything that can help me can help anybody.

Pamper yourself. When you're going through recovery, you need to go through a season of simply pampering yourself. Take hot baths, get a massage, buy yourself something you really enjoy. Forget about your budget for a while and start loving yourself. David encouraged himself in the Lord. Encourage yourself: Get a manicure, get a pedicure, find a cure, do something! Brothers, send your wives to the beauty salon, or just send their hair and let the wives stay home (just kidding!). Go to a good movie, take a trip, go to a fine restaurant. Love yourself for a season. When you do this, don't worry about anyone else for a while. Learn how to make yourself happy. You're worth it. Now, go on and bless yourself!

Guard your emotional mental health by being kind to yourself. Stay away from toxic things, toxic situations, and toxic people for a season. Take your time. Don't over extend yourself, don't try to understand everything, and don't try to figure everything out. Just go out and bless yourself. I'm not talking about running up credit cards. We need balance, because anything that doesn't have balance has demons.

I promise you that you will begin to feel good about yourself again. You will be able to "jumpstart" your body and your brain again, and your emotional healing will begin to take place. If you don't love yourself, watch how many years it will take before you come out of your situation. Remember: Love yourself!

Chapter Twenty-One

Self-Image

"I am fearfully and wonderfully made!"
Psalm 139:14

From the day that you were born, the devil has been attempting to destroy your self-image. Unfortunately, we have a society that tries to tell us what's beautiful and what's intelligent. Their perceptions are in front of us all of the time. This can be self-destructive in that we can feel that we're not living up to a necessary "standard," feeling we're not living up to what society deems adequate.

I don't care how much money you make or where you live; it doesn't matter what you drive, or the extent of your education, but if you die leaving a broken, dysfunctional family, you are a failure. You cannot tell God you are a success because you have 80 trillion dollars in the bank, when you've been divorced three or four times and your children are wayward. God will measure your success by what shape your family is in after you're gone. The Bible says, "The memory of the just is blessed" (Proverbs 10:7). In other words, when you're gone, people still remember you and say, "That was a great man," or "That was a great woman." You will be remembered most for your greatest obsession.

Success has nothing to do with dollars. Howard Hughes proved that. He virtually owned everything in Las Vegas, but he died a recluse. True love brings you happiness. If you've got someone who loves you like Christ loved the Church, then no matter what else you are without, you can deal with it.

We are what we believe we are. That is a very simple, but complex, truth. Dr. Maxwell Maltz, a psychologist, wrote, "The goal of any psychotherapy is to change an individual's image of himself." God has the same problem with us. He's trying to mold us into His image, by way of the Holy Spirit. You cannot see yourself as a victim and be victorious.

Sometimes, as Black people, we still see ourselves as slaves, whether we want to be honest about it or not. When we are feeling good about ourselves, other people seem very nice. When we hate ourselves, we hate everyone else. When we love being who we are, the rest of the world is wonderful. Our self-image is the blueprint that tells exactly how we will behave, who we will mix with, what we will try, and what we will avoid. Our every thought and action stems from the way we see ourselves.

There are many Black people who won't go into affluent neighborhoods, neither would you shop in the better stores. You see yourself as a poverty-stricken person, almost to the point of saying to yourself, "I'm not worthy to go in there." You won't say it with your conscious mind, but these thoughts are taking place in your subconscious. Whose report will you believe? If I'm a joint heir with Jesus, that says something! It's impossible to really read and meditate on what you read in the Bible and continue to maintain a poor self-image.

If the streets of Heaven are made of gold, that shows you what God thinks about you. Whoever heard of a king that doesn't have a kingdom. If he has a kingdom, then he ought to have servants. Whoever heard of a king without a treasury? You can't be a king without money. So, if I'm a joint-heir with the King of all kings, shouldn't I have some of His gold? I ought to have some of His diamonds and His treasury!!

You are what you attract. If mess is attracted to you, then you need to change your self-image. You are what the Word says you should be. Even if you aren't saved, you ought to have a healthy self-image. The picture we have of ourselves is colored by our experiences -- by our successes and our failures. The thoughts that we have had about ourselves and other people have an effect upon us in many ways. When we believe this image to be a fact, we begin to live and operate within the bounds of the mental picture our minds have drawn. You may not want to believe this, but if you grew up in a "put-down" environment that was hostile to who you are as a person, and all you know is hostility, then you were trained not to like yourself.

Our self-image determines how much we like the world and whether we feel worthy to enjoy living in it. Self-image also determines how much we will accomplish in life. The first step towards a vast improvement in our effectiveness is to change the way we think and talk about ourselves. Our self-image is like a thermostat and we continue to perform within the prescribed range.

We decide on our own self-image. People can suggest things to us, but the ultimate choice is our own. It's mom and dad's job to mold a strong, healthy self-image while you are young. It's not your teacher's responsibility, and it's not even your pastor's responsibility. The responsibility first rests with your mom and dad. They should have been telling you that you can do anything that you put your mind to. Daddies should have picked up their daughters in their arms and told them how pretty they are. Some young ladies had to hear they were pretty by some fellow on the street. We call the young, promiscuous women we see today "hot-tails," but they're really suffering from an "emotional void" which is a vacuum in their lives. They're not loose; they're hungry for emotional support. Parents may beat their daughters, calling them sluts, while the real problem is that your job as a parent has been left undone.

I have nine children. All of them aren't as intelligent as the next. It's no effort for one of my daughters to get straight A's. I've got a son who's struggling to get straight C's. I watch him. When my daughter brings her report card in, she's happy to give it to me. But, he's standing back in the corner, hoping to God I don't ask for it, but he knows I don't want him suffering from shame either. When I get his report card, I tell him, "Now, you know you can do better." I tell him, "Son, study a little more. You can do it." He looks at me and says, "I can?" I tell him, "Yes, you can! You're smart. You're very intelligent."

Life balances itself out. The people who were getting so far ahead when you were in high school, those who seemed they would be the most successful, haven't succeeded as far as you thought. Surprisingly, the ones who have succeeded are the ones who you didn't even consider. When they discovered what was within them, and built up a healthy self-image, they took off. I've found out that people who I thought were born with silver spoons in their mouths can hardly even buy a spoon now. Some of them don't even know how to use one! You don't have to worry about people getting ahead of you. God has a way of moving you up to pass that person that seemingly goes so far ahead of you.

I found out that my job is to discover who I am and be that person perfectly.

If anyone has a problem with that, then "Later, 'Gator." All I know to be is me. I've got to be true to what I am. You aren't going to get along with everyone, even when you're saved. The saints in the Bible didn't always get along. Paul and Barnabas almost went to blows over John Mark, according to the Book of Acts. The saints may not get along, but it doesn't mean that they don't love one another. It just means that we sometimes have personality conflicts. This is especially true of people who have the gift of government because they can be very bossy.

We decide our own self-image. I've yet to see a Black man or Black woman advertise in a health club commercial or a cologne commercial. I'm not trying to perpetuate racism, but I'm trying to destroy a bad self-image. I don't allow my children to play with anything but Black dolls, because a child will begin to interject his or her own personality into that doll, and vice versa. You always seek the approval of people that intimidate you. Too many of us have gone to a certain race of people for validation. When you think you've got their validation, you try to live up to it by putting your own people down. If you want someone's validation, then God bless you, but don't come back with an arrogant attitude. Just because I don't talk, walk, or act like those you think validated you, you want to put me down. And, you haven't really gotten their approval because they haven't invited you over for dinner yet, and you won't be marrying their daughter either.

Part of my job as a man of God is to straighten out sin, and being a respecter of persons, my Bible says, is sin. That's why we are out here killing each other in unprecedented numbers. The carnage among Black people is at epidemic proportions, all because we don't love ourselves. There's no way one brother loves another brother when you're out here blowing him away or sticking him up, selling dope, or breaking in his home. You don't love me and don't call me a brother. You're stealing my car, abusing my daughters, and you call me a brother? You're a liar. Brothers don't treat one another like that. We've got to change the self-image of a race of people and it needs to start in the church. We've got to make the change by first admitting that the problem exists.

We decide our own worth and we also decide how much happiness to expect. Being egotistical and having a healthy self-image are complete opposites. People with huge egos need to be the center of attention. They crave recognition and have little concern for those around them. Surely, we can be proud of our achievements without feeling the need to broadcast them. When we genuinely appreciate our own worth, there's no need to tell the world that "I'm this" or "I'm that" or announce your worth to everyone you meet. It is the person who has to convince himself of his own worth who has a need to inform everyone else, too.

We form relationships with people who treat us the way we believe we deserve to be treated. If you have a poor self-image, you put up with all kinds of garbage and abuse from just about anyone. People treat us the way we treat ourselves. Those with whom we associate quickly assess whether or not we respect ourselves. If we treat ourselves with respect, they will follow suit. Patterns of abuse will continue until you decide on or demand fair treatment from friends, relatives, co-workers, saints, and everyone else. When you take a stand, people will honor that. The bottom line is that when you have a healthy self-image, nobody's running over you, because you love yourself.

Brothers, what happens when you see someone "dissing" (disrespecting) your mother? You say, "Hey, man, you don't talk like that to my momma. You don't treat her like that." Well, why don't you feel that way about yourself? Thank God you feel that way about your mother, but why not feel the same way about people mistreating you? When you have a healthy self-image, you won't tolerate people using vulgar language around you, especially you ladies. You will stop them in their tracks.

You may think that's an "uppity" attitude, but I just know what garbage is. I have a revelation of "trash." You should demand respect, and, when you do, people will respect you. People will test you, also. Husbands and wives test one another to see what they can get away with. People are constantly testing you to see if you have a healthy self-image. You'd be surprised how the people you meet will size you, up and down. They start thinking, "Are they well-off, educated, low class? What are they?" I've discovered that people will usually try to bring you down to the level they're on when they are "lower" than you are. When people are "higher" than you are, they usually don't want to be bothered with you. If you have a healthy self-image, you will think of yourself as an eagle and fly above what they are trying to do.

Patterns of abuse will continue until we decide and expect

to receive fair treatment from people. You can be sure that everyone knows when they cannot run over you and you will hear it. You will be called and accused of being "uppity." Black people will be accused of "trying to be White." If White is being self-respected, then call me Snow White!! Some people like being low and have no dreams or ambitions about rising up. Leave people like this alone, or you can expect to be carrying them. They will be parasites on you. That, again, is co-dependency. "Can you help me out? Can you give me? You seem to be doing so well."

The best thing you can do for a poor person is to not be one of them. Whatever you do for them won't be enough. There's no sense in both of you being on welfare. Don't get me wrong. I enjoy helping people who want help. These are the easiest people to minister to. But people who don't want help are a waste of time. You can't try to talk business with someone who doesn't want to understand business. People want your gift, but they are not willing to pay the price that you had to pay to get it. Then, they want to drag you down because you paid the price and are advancing over them. A healthy self-image will warn you of parasites. A rich man has many friends.

POOR SELF-IMAGE TRAITS

There are many poor self-image traits that we should be aware of and that we should avoid. Following is a list of some poor self-image traits. Some of them we will discuss in detail:

1) **Jealousy**
2) **Negative self-talk about yourself**
3) **Guilt**
4) **Failure to give compliments and non-acceptance of**

compliments

A poor self-image will prevent you from complimenting anyone. Do you remember when the last time was that you went out of your way to compliment someone? Why do you feel you are the only one that can dress well? We should encourage one another. People can compliment you and you will tell them they are lying and think they want something. If a brother compliments some sisters, they immediately think he wants to go to bed with them. Many women have problems in this area. These men don't always want to date you, they just want to be gentlemen...well, sometimes.

5) Not taking care of your own needs
6) Failure to give affection
7) Inability to receive and enjoy affection
You can marry into a situation where the person with a low self-image has never been loved before. It's hard for them to handle this. They can't hold hands walking down the street and don't like any type of public affection.

8) Criticism of others
I was in a buffet restaurant one day, and the person I was with began criticizing the food and everyone in the restaurant. "This is just bad food. And look at the people around here. They are all just so fat." This person railed the people so bad in that restaurant that it unnerved me. This person had a lot of nerve looking down at people. But, I remember some things about this person as a child. This person was quite hefty. "The thing you don't like in another person is usually

the thing you don't like in yourself."

Most poor people are overweight because they eat the wrong foods, not necessarily because they overeat. They can't afford to eat "high fiber" or "low fat" foods all the time because these foods can be costly. When you're poor, there's no such thing as "breakfast food." Food is food. You're just glad something is in front of you. We're so blessed here in America that we can choose to say what foods we will eat at certain times of the day. But, when you are poor, it's another story. You eat whatever, without thoughts of content. You're just grateful that SOMETHING is on the table!

9) Comparison of yourself with others
(The Bible warns constantly against comparing yourself with other people.)

10) Constant poor health
You're not taking care of yourself. People with a healthy self-image will take care of themselves and will not allow themselves to just waste away.

Men usually have more of a problem with this than women do. Men do not like taking care of themselves. If your wife thinks she's sick, she will run to the hospital. With a man, it is a different story. That's why men need good wives to help take care of them.

Women, don't marry men who won't let them go to the beauty salon. It takes work to look pretty, and it takes work to be handsome. If you can't be handsome, at least be neat. I've seen the ugliest of people who were very neat and it made a difference in their appearance. Poor health can be a result of poor self-image. Take care of yourself. When you don't care about yourself, you don't take care of yourself. If you can take care of your teeth at the dentist, you can take care of your feet. Most men don't care about their nails and their feet. Women look at your nails, they look at your teeth – they look everywhere. Wives ought to encourage your husbands when he goes to the dentist. Likewise, my brother, it's important to encourage your wife to take care of herself. Did you not know it is therapeutic for a woman to take care of herself? It is needful for a woman to go to the beauty salon. It is needful that women get their nails and toes painted. It's a necessity. You need to maximize upon the beauty with which God has blessed you. It took my wife years to get me to go and get a pedicure. I thought it was "sissy" stuff. But, one day I went and it relaxed me so much that I fell asleep.

You may have to make changes and adjustments in your life to combat a poor self-image. And, change is difficult. The reaction of a poor self-image is to help perpetuate itself. Do you need to change your image? If you won't do it for anybody, do it for yourself. It's all about feeling good about yourself. The better you feel about yourself, the better you will relate to other people.

Some of the angriest people today are people that don't like themselves. The men and women who are being "dogged-out" is not necessarily because their spouses are bad. There are some men who quickly assess how they can "get over" on the women with whom they enter into a relationship, based on what she will allow him to do. Whether you want to believe this or not, there are women who act the same way. A real man is not going to let you run over him, and a real lady is not going to let you mistreat her. Don't complain about what you permit. You are in control of your own destiny and it's tied into your self-image.

When you see yourself successful, you will be successful. If you think you can't do something, you can't. Be around people who celebrate you, not tolerate you. When you can control what comes into your mind, then you can control what comes into your hands.

Chapter Twenty-Two

Maturity - Not Comparing Yourself to Others

*If you learn something from
a life experience, it was not a mistake!*

BEING HAPPY

Are you happy? I'm going to mess up some "Word of Faith" teaching by sharing with you some biblical truths about happiness. God has nothing to do with your being happy or unhappy. Being unhappy is not a sin. I don't know of a child of God who has not experienced some time of unhappiness in their life. If your prayer is "God, make me happy," He won't do it. That isn't His job any more than it is to make you get saved. I don't know of anyone who God dragged out into the street, into the House of the Lord, and made them come to the altar, demanding that they get saved. I'm sensationalizing a little bit, because I want to build a foundation in your thinking upon which to build the truth.

Over 100 years ago, Abraham Lincoln said that most people are about as happy as they make up their minds to be. Christians look to life and expect life to make them happy. But, you don't arrive at happiness in the same way that you arrive at a bus stop. Happiness, first and foremost, is a decision, and if we have happiness in our lives, it is because we chose it.

The life that most people are experiencing is really one of "existence." That is the type of life we are speaking of when we say that life is unfair. That kind of life will disappoint you so badly that you almost feel like giving up. The church is full of unhappy folks who haven't executed their right to choose properly. As much as God has done for us, we don't have a right to be unhappy.

The god of this world has blinded people's minds (II Corinthians 4:3,4). He has deceived them into believing that the allurement and possession of money, power, and pleasure can bring them happiness. But, do those things really bring you happiness? The news is replete with stories of ultra-rich individuals who are in a state of extreme unhappiness in their lives. Many of us are unhappy because our expectations about life have let us down. Happiness is generally predicated by circumstances, and when your circumstances change, your happiness will change.

Trying to obtain happiness in this life is an exercise in futility, if you think that it can be obtained by living in a certain place, or earning a particular sum of money, or driving that dream car. We think that if we can just have something, we will be happy. That's not what the Bible says. Jesus said, "I am the Way, the Truth, and the Life" (John 14:6). If you really want to experience life, get born again, and Jesus will give you the more abundant life (John 10:10).

It is not what happens in life that determines our happiness so much as it is the way that we react to what happens to us. For example, one man loses his job. He says,

"Oh, God, how am I going to feed my family? How am I going to pay the bills? How am I going to pay for the car?" His self-esteem is destroyed and he shuts the door upon himself as he goes into his room to have a pity-party. Another man loses his job with the same company. He says, "Oh, bless His Holy Name! I was asking God to deliver me from this job. I have a car note, a house note, and children to feed. In all of this, the Lord is my Shepherd, and I shall not want." It's how you respond to these things that make you happy or unhappy. One guy wants to die, and the other guy is pressing on.

If you live long enough, you will find out the real deal about life. You're going to have to tell life that you don't care what it throws at you, for you're still pressing on. If you're waiting for life to change and make you happy, you might as well go and make an appointment right now at the funeral parlor. It isn't. Jesus said that you'd better come to Him because that other life that you thought was life is disappointing: "Come unto Me all ye that labor..." (Matthew 11:28). Who are these laboring folks? Folks who are laboring to be happy, laboring to make enough money, laboring to obtain an opulent lifestyle, and laboring to get out of the ghetto to the "get-mo." All laboring is vain. Life will throw you for a loop. In life, you go from one mountaintop to another, but in between the mountaintops, you've got to go down into the valley. We all like the mountaintops, but no one cares for the experiences in the valley.

I know people who have observed and studied the laws of success, who have done everything right and still fail. You're a law-abiding citizen, you praise and worship God, and you pay tithes. But, you still get "thrown for a loop." You can treat everybody right and folks will still "diss" you. You can love everybody and still have enemies. Why…because that's what life is all about. Life is a "trip."

If you don't come to Jesus, life will defeat you. Someone once said, "Life is not fair, but God evens the score." David said, "my familiar friends who sat at my table have lifted up their heels against me" (Psalm 41.9). David was getting a picture of life when it isn't treating you right. But with Jesus, you get that more abundant life. David said, "When my father and mother forsake me, then the Lord will take me up" (Psalm 27:10).

We decide how we act in life, even when we lost control. Decisions that you make can be the basis for your happiness or unhappiness. Being happy isn't always easy. I want to get right down to some things, beloved. You're unhappy because you want to be. You just make yourself unhappy. Proverbs 23:7 says, "For as he thinketh in his heart, so is he."

Maturity means taking responsibility for your own happiness and choosing to concentrate on what we've got rather than what we haven't got. There are about three or four classifications of unhappy people, but the most unhappy people I've found are the one's comparing themselves with somebody. That will not only make you unhappy, it will make you miserable.

You don't know how folks got what they have. Some folks backslide to get it and you're looking at them unhappily because you don't have it. Are you willing to backslide? Other folks pay a dear price to get what they have. Are you willing to pay that price? Quit looking at someone else. The Joneses are not your norm. You look at others and think, "Oh, boy, look at him. He just has everything. I wonder how many more cars he's going to get. I don't have my first yet. I have to take a bus home." Well, at least, you can walk to the bus. I'm reminded of a story about a guy who said he used to feel sorry for himself because he didn't have any shoes, until he found a man who didn't have any feet!

Are you comparing yourself with someone? The police department as well as psychologists say that, generally, the holidays are the most unhappy time of year for a lot of people. Folks are under the impression that you've got to have somebody. But, we fail to realize that Jesus was the greatest single person that there ever was. If having someone brings happiness, then talk to some divorced folks. They will tell you, "I had something, but I had nothing." Some of the folks you are looking at, that you think are so happy, are just wearing masks. God is trying to do you a favor, and you're getting miserable because you think you need someone. You think that you're unhappy now? You'd better count your blessings! During the Christmas season, people are down, thinking, "I don't have anyone to toast with by the fireplace" or "I don't have anyone to kiss under the mistletoe." God sometimes has to separate to educate. Half of the people you're looking at are not happy. Sometimes that man is just with that woman because he realizes that "it's cheaper to keep her."

That's why you need Jesus, beloved. Listen, I want money. I want the things that I've worked for, but I don't want them to make me happy. That's how folks get killed. If your happiness is in things, it can be destroyed. If damage comes to the physical object of someone's happiness, they will want to kill you. You can get killed faster by hitting a man's car than hitting his wife: "You hit my car. You tore up my happiness. Don't mess with my happiness or else you will die." He looks for that car to bring him happiness.

Did you ever get wrapped up into something that you thought was so crucial to your happiness? I promise you, if you love anything more than God, God will allow it to be destroyed. Anything you love more than God will be taken away. Is that why you're unhappy today? Is it because your "god" was destroyed? And, don't stay unhappy because of the loss. God says, "I'm a jealous God" (Exodus 2:5, paraphrased). "My name is Jealous" (Exodus 34:14). I repeat: Anything you love more than God, or anything you worship more than God, is an idol, and He will allow it to be destroyed. Sometimes our little idols of the heart get destroyed during the course of life and we become unhappy. But, a lot of things you're unhappy about losing today were taking you to hell. God in His wisdom knows what He is doing, but sometimes we stay angry about what was taken from us.

There are some things that God lets the devil do. See, the devil does serve a purpose. God permits the devil to destroy things. If the devil did something, it was by God's permission. You may wonder why God wants you unhappy. He doesn't, but you should be happy in everything. That's what the word "delight" means. If you lost something, and that which you lost caused you to lose the joy of your salvation, I promise you that God allowed that thing to be destroyed. I doubt very seriously if you are saved if that loss caused you to lose the joy of your salvation. Man looks to the corner, but God sees around the corner. He sees that this thing that you have isn't going to bring you much joy or bring Him glory. So, He asks for it. But if you don't want to give it to God, He says, "Fine. Where's that devil?" God steps out of the way and lets the devil tear it up. Your car just got wrecked and you wonder why. If it was an idol, God knows that two years from now you would have been picking up a lot of strange women or you, sister, would let strange men into your car. You may be unhappy about it now, not understanding why God let it happen. But God says He's looking at eternal value here. If necessary, He'd rather you are unhappy for ten years than to spend all of eternity in hell. That's the wisdom of God.

We control our own happiness as we decide the thoughts we think. "As a man thinketh, so is he" (Proverbs 23:7). So, to be happy, we need to concentrate on happy thoughts. Most people that are unhappy are thinking unhappy thoughts, and you are what you think. The devil has you thinking on things that aren't edifying, but Philippians 4:8 admonishes us:

> *"Finally brother, whatsoever things are true, whatsoever things are honest, whatsoever things are just, whatsoever things are pure, whatsoever things are lovely, whatsoever things are of a good report, if there be any virtue, and if there be any praise, think on these things."*

Look at all of the people walking around during Thanksgiving and Christmas with their lips dragging on their shoe tops because they're thinking about what it is going to feel like to be alone. It hasn't even happened yet. But, just the idea of being this way has depressed them. What you actually experience might not even be as bad as you imagine it will be, but you've convinced yourself that it's so. It's just like when you were small and your momma and daddy promised you a whipping. The thought of it was fearful, but after it happened, it wasn't so bad.

"Whatsoever things are good, and true, think on these things" (Philippians 4:8, paraphrased). And, "Whose report are you going to believe?" (Isaiah 53:1, paraphrased). The entire time that the devil is talking negatively to you, I believe that God is trying to get a good report in there. I refuse to believe that the devil is out-talking God. But, they tell me, the dog you feed the most is going to have the loudest bark.

What we believe is what we decide to believe. We just want to believe negative things. You want to believe you're going down the tubes, that you will never be with anyone, that you're going to die, that your disease is terminal, that you'll never succeed, that nobody likes you, and that you're ugly and won't ever find anybody. YOU WANT TO BELIEVE THIS! The bad thing about it is that most unhappy people will try to perpetuate their negative thoughts to make you unhappy.

If we allow a bad experience or a nasty remark to occupy our mind, we will suffer the consequences. One of the keys of life is not allowing bad experiences to get on the inside of you because they can affect how you think. Then, they can become "MIND-SETS.' If they stay there long enough, they can become strongholds. Is there a stronghold in your mind that you need to tear down?

Psychologists state, "that you gravitate and move toward the most dominant thoughts in your mind." Many of the thoughts that come to your mind are not from God. We do receive thoughts from the Holy Spirit, but also from our own human spirit, and then there's the devil himself. Now, when you've got the Word of God in you, or have a good idea what the Word says; and when a thought comes in that does not line up with the Word of God, the Bible instructs us to cast it down. If we don't cast it down, it will become a mind-set and, as stated previously, eventually a stronghold. Every time we look at you, you will look like you bathed in lemon-juice. This is a common problem for unhappy people in the Body of Christ. Not only do we move toward our dominant thoughts, but also we will eventually act out our dominant thoughts. If the devil wants to control us, he usually does it through suggestion. He suggests what you should be unhappy about and he will have you looking at other people, comparing your happiness with theirs.

Now, why doesn't he have you comparing yourself with someone in Nigeria or India or other places in the third world. I've visited these third world nations, and I can tell you that if you were to go there, you would come back rejoicing. You would be delighted to get back to America. Most of you don't have any idea how the rest of the world is living. If you did, you would be content where you are. What you do have is more than most people in the world. You say you don't have much? With whom are you comparing yourself?

Many of the single men and women today are unhappy because they aren't married. Part of the reason that you aren't married is because you're comparing yourself with someone who is. So, what if you know someone who got married at twenty-one years old? You don't know why God had that person get married so young. And, you don't know if when they got married, it was the will of God. I'd rather get married at forty years old and stay married, than get married at twenty-one and be divorced at twenty-one and a half.

When God shows up, He knows how to make up for lost time. If someone is taking a long time in the kitchen, you know they're preparing a good meal. Now, honey, do you want a meal or a snack? God must really be cooking something great for you. Let God have His way.

Most people remember compliments for a few minutes, but remember insults for years. If no one ever told you that you were beautiful, you ought to know it for yourself. Some folks just don't appreciate beauty. There's no point in becoming unhappy about it. That's what gives some people the ability to create wealth – they are able to see things that others cannot see. If everyone saw exactly the same thing, then we would all be rich. What happens to poor people is that they don't have a revelation of some things. Remember, "Jesus went among His own, and His own received Him not" (John 1:11, paraphrased).

Being happy is like maintaining a nice home. You've got to throw out the garbage, but keep the treasures. When negative thoughts come to your mind that are garbage, throw them out. When those nuggets and rhemas come from the Lord, hold on to them; they are treasures. Someone once asked me, "Apostle, what can I do about these negative thoughts?" You can't control the birds that fly over your house, but you can control those who make a nest there!

Many of you are unhappy because you're thinking about mess. You refuse to let go of that mess in your mind; and you won't release that messed up situation the devil continues to bring in your thoughts. It's not only having an effect on your mental psyche, but it's having an effect on your attitude.

Some of the saints' attitudes STINK! Gifted, but no character. Anointed, but no character. You just finished worshipping God and speaking in tongues, but now you aren't even friendly. I don't understand how you can come out of the "Presence of God" and be so rude as to not even speak to one another – the saints. They will walk right past one another, or look you in the face and not even speak to you. If you don't initiate a "Good morning" or a "Praise the Lord, they will walk right past you. Before I had the Holy Ghost, my momma taught me some manners.

Sometimes bad attitudes come from being unhappy. When you are unhappy, nobody wants to be around you because you're a "sour puss." God designed your face to be happy. It takes more muscles to frown than to smile, but it's YOUR decision to smile, not His. He presents the opportunity for us to be happy; He shows us the way out; and when we don't understand it, He says, "Come unto me, all ye that labor and are heavy laden, and I will give you rest" (Matthew 11:28). And the Bible also says, "Call unto me and I will answer thee and show thee great and mighty things which thou knowest not" (Jeremiah 33:3).

Being happy requires looking for good things. You choose what you see, and you choose what you think. It's your choice. Haven't you had enough misery? Haven't you had enough headaches, heartaches, and loneliness? Now, it's time for you to change all of this. Just choose. Happiness is your choice. It starts with the thoughts you want to think; it starts with the things you want to believe; and it starts with the reality you believe you're going to have. If you really believe you're getting a harvest when you release seed, you'd be jumping up and down. In fact, you'd tell people in front of you to move so you won't hit them in the back. But most people are unhappy when they give because they're listening to the devil. The devil tells them, "Man, how are you going to do this? How are you going to pay for this?" Things will not work out the way you fear they will. Believing your fears is called "stinking thinking." Get rid of it and decide to be happy!!

The happy-smiley stickers on the back of cars is the world's way of telling you, "Don't worry, be happy." The world is even teaching folks not to think about negative things because worry is the misuse of imagination. Worry is mental malpractice. You are temporarily insane when you start worrying. Worry will send you right to a mental institution when all you have to do is look up (to God) before you "crack-up!"

You need a good, healthy sense of humor. The Lord told me, "Cliff, it's not that serious." Watch people that are unhappy. They don't have a sense of humor. I am so glad God has graced me with a sense of humor. When you laugh, endorphins are leased in your brain which give you a natural high, and you give your respiratory system a good workout, just like you would get if you were jogging. Laughter, beloved, relieves pain. You can only laugh when you're relaxed, and the more relaxed you are, the less pain you will feel. Find something to laugh at. Looking at someone with a funny face. Check your mirror! (Just kidding!)

Just like with a remote control, we change channels when watching a bad movie. We don't give TV programs a long time to convince us that they're interesting. We'll change the channel if we don't like the music, the introduction, or the characters. If there isn't anything interesting on the other channels, we cut off the TV, and find something else to do. It's the same thing with your mind. It shouldn't take you long to find out the thing that the devil's trying to bring to your mind isn't edifying. Just like the remote control, you can turn to the next channel. You say to yourself, "Don't look at this or think on that, it's going to make me unhappy." It's the same thing with the radio. If you listen to certain music, it isn't going to build you up. Music can remind you of something from your past that hurt you. From the time you get up in the morning to the time you go to bed, the devil is ram-rodding your mind with thoughts and suggestions from every means possible that will ultimately make you miserable. When he does, it is your job to change the channel.

If you are unhappy today, it means that you have not taken control of the thoughts in your mind. You don't have any excuse for being unhappy. If you're unhappy, it's because you choose to believe the devil's report. What the devil shows you will always discourage you. You've got to make up in your mind that circumstances aren't that bad and choose not to think on them. Often, just when you decide not to think about negative things, someone talking to you will try to bring negative things your way. You must learn to train people how to talk to you.

People will ask you about negative things over which you've already taken authority and cast down. If they ask, "Whatever happened to so and so?" or "What are you doing about this?" Tell them, "I'm not dwelling on that today. For this is the day that the Lord has made and today, I said I was going to rejoice; not become worried, perplexed, or melancholy. This day I'm rejoicing. Now, is there something else you want to talk about?"

What are you thinking on now that's trying to make you unhappy. Even if you are thinking about something you really don't want to think on, you will find yourself dismissing it from your mind and then gravitating towards it again. The mind moves towards things. This is why the Lord wants you to put Him on your mind. "A mind stayed on Him will keep you in perfect peace" (Isaiah 26:3 paraphrased, emphasis added).

Not only do you have to choose what you're going to think about; you also have to be careful about images. Images create desire. The devil tries to plant negative and sinful images in your mind. The Bible warns us to cast them down. God understands how the devil likes playing with your mind. He will also use people to get to you. You're familiar with the ones who are always playing mind games with you. The worst enemies you have are those who play mind games with you. You sometimes want to kill someone who's playing with your mind. When your heart gets broken, you want to cry; but when your mind snaps...folks start looking to put you in the nut house.

The mind is a tremendous instrument, and the devil understands how it operates. Happiness is just a decision. You should tell life, "I don't care what happens; I'm still going to rejoice." Let happiness be your decision. Don't base it upon what you see, but base your happiness upon the Word of God. I choose to be happy, because I trust God. I don't trust life, but I trust God. If life doesn't do me right, I don't run to life, I run to Jesus. "Many are the afflictions of the righteous, but the Lord delivereth him out of them all" (Psalm 34:19). Pull off that sad face and put on a garment of praise for the spirit of heaviness, and lift up the Name of Jesus!

The broken become masters at healing. You are the people whom God wants to use to heal His people because the broken always become masters at healing. You are the first partaker of the fruit. You can't heal what you can't feel.

Your misery is your ministry. The thing that caused you hurt, pain, and repression is the thing that God wants you to warn others with wisdom and with an anointing and heal them. Minister effectively to them.

It is my prayer and sincerest desire that this book has helped in your journey towards recovery.

Beware of blindspots ...

unhealed wounds, unchallenged beliefs.

When you refuse to change,

you wind up in chains!

RECOVERY TEST #4
(Includes review questions from previous chapters. Answer key in Appendix A)

1) WHEN YOU LOVE YOURSELF TOO MUCH, YOU CAN BECOME:

masochistic
narcissistic
pessimistic

2)   WHAT ARE THE THREE TYPES OF LOVE?

a)
b)
c)

3)_____ means God's unconditional love.

CIRCLE "T" FOR TRUE AND "F" FOR FALSE FOR THE FOLLOWING:

4)   T   F   If you don't love yourself enough, you will develop low self-esteem.

5)   T   F   If you're not loving yourself, you are in sin.

6)   T   F   I John 4:8 says, "For God is love.".

7)   T   F   One of the many reasons why God tells us not to have any fellowship with unbelievers is because a nonbeliever doesn't have a revelation of love.

8)   T   F   One does not need professional help or any other outside help to get through grief if he/she is saved. God is all we need.

SHORT ANSWERS:

9) Why is it important not to take on new responsibilities when you're recovering from emotional hurts?

10) Is it wise to enter into a relationship with a person who's been through hurt? Why or why not?

11) Why is rekindling old relationships the biggest mistake you can make when coming out of a bad situation?

12) Why is it important to have a good (saved) friend (of the same sex) to talk to before getting involved again?

13) What does drinking water have to do with healing in your body?

14) The way out of grief is going _____.

15) What is one of life's most valuable lessons?

16) In letting go, you have to choose <u>being happy</u> over …

17) List five things discussed in this manual to help us get through grief.

1.

2.

3.

4.

5.

CIRCLE "T" FOR TRUE AND "F" FOR FALSE FOR THE FOLLOWING:

18)　　T　　F　　When you are angry with someone, you are chained to that offense. You are chained to them in your memory.

19)　　T　　F　　It is possible to wait grief out.

20)　　T　　F　　Negative thinking is mental malpractice.

21)　　T　　F　　It is possible to let go (mentally) of a bad relationship even if you see yourself as a victim.

22)   T   F   Blame and guilt will distract you from your real purpose in God.

23)   T   F   Our self-image is the blueprint that tells exactly how we will behave, who we will mix with, what we will try, and what we will avoid.

24)   T   F   Our self-image does not necessarily determine how much we will accomplish in life.

LIST 5 OUT OF 10 POOR SELF-IMAGE TRAITS DISCUSSED IN THIS SECTION.

1.

2.

3.

4.

5.

Appendix A: Answer Keys

RECOVERY TEST #1 ANSWER KEY
(Answers are in bold and italics)

1) WHAT ARE THE FIRST STAGES OF RECOVERY

    a) fear, anger, depression
    b) shock, denial, numbness
    c) understanding, acceptance, moving on

2) WHAT ARE THE SECOND STAGES OF RECOVERY

    a) fear, anger, depression
    b) shock, denial, numbness
    c) understanding, acceptance, moving on

3) HOW IS DEPRESSION BROUGHT ON?
    a) suppressed anger
    b) suppressed fear
    c) grieving over a loved one
    d) one, two, or all three of the above

4) WHAT ARE THE LAST STAGES OF RECOVERY
    a) fear, anger, depression
    b) shock, denial, numbness
    c) understanding, acceptance, moving on

5) GOING INTO EMOTIONAL SHOCK AFTER A TRAUMATIC EVENT THE PERSON BECOMES NUMB. ONCE NUMBNESS SUBSIDES, EMOTIONS RETURN. THIS IS CALLED:

    a) Hitting Rock Bottom
    b) Chronic Shock Syndrome
    c) Processing Your Anger

CIRCLE "T" FOR TRUE AND "F" FOR FALSE FOR THE FOLLOWING:

6)   T   F   A person with a character disorder assumes too much responsibility; They say they have a problem.

7)   T   F   A neurotic doesn't assume enough responsibility; they don't see themselves as having a problem.

8)   T   F   When anger is turned inward it causes depression.

9)   T   F   When anger is turned outward it causes unforgiveness.

10)   T   F   Anger gets you in trouble, but pride keeps you there.

11)   T   F   Repression is anger turned inside.

12)   T   F   It is impossible to work anger out of you.

13)   T   F   Shame is when someone or something causes us disgrace.

14)   T   F   Loneliness is not an absence of direction, it is an absence of affection.

15)   T   F   Anger usually is the result of people's needs not getting met.

16)   T   F   "Hitting rock bottom" is a phrase used to describe repression.

17) **T**   **F**   Unreconciled loneliness will eventually move a person to a season of depression.

CIRCLE THE CORRECT LETTER FOR THE FOLLOWING:

18)   When your sensitivity is worn down, when a foundation for immoral behavior is instilled, and isolation occurs, this indicates the stages of:

   a) fear, anger, depression
   b) shock, denial, numbness
   c) understanding, acceptance, moving on

19)   What Book of the Bible shows the ups and downs?

   a) Ecclesiastes
   b) Song of Solomon
   c) Psalms

20)   Most people who are hurt go through a time of complaining and feelings of self-pity, otherwise known as:

   a) The Lying Syndrome
   b) The Elijah Syndrome
   c) The Eli Syndrome

21)   What are the two things that abort healing/deliverance in your life?

   a) anger and unforgiveness
   b) fear and unforgiveness
   c) pride and unforgiveness

FILL IN THE BLANK:

Another name for "tormentors" according to Matthew 18 is _____*demons*_____.

SHORT ANSWER:

23)   Explain what "psychosomatic" means.

How you think affects your body. Diseases are connected with your mind.

RECOVERY TEST #2 ANSWER KEY
(Answers are in bold and italics)

1)   WHAT IS "BURNOUT"?
        a) a depletion of energy and a feeling of being overwhelmed
        b) a condition wherein you cannot keep up with your usual round of activities
        c) a syndrome of emotional exhaustion
        d) all of the above
        e) none of the above

2) PEOPLE WHO HAVE "BURNOUT" ARE USUALLY:
        a) people who feel they need to prove something to others
        b) people who put a lot of pressure on themselves
        c) people who don't allow time for outside activities
        d) all of the above
        e) none of the above

3) PEOPLE WHO ARE CO-DEPENDENT:
a) require another individual for sound survival
b) feel they "need" somebody to live
c) a only
d) b only
e) both a and b

4) PASSIVELY DEPENDENT PEOPLE:
a) tolerate loneliness very well
b) have a possessive spirit
c) have no real sense of identity
d) both a and b
e) both b and c

MULTIPLE CHOICE: SELECT THE APPROPRIATE LETTER IN THE BLANK ON THE LEFT

a) Job Burn-out; b) Mental Burn-out; c) Physical Burn-out;
   d) Spiritual Burn-out

5)___**B**____ Results from feeling frustrated by a sense of helplessness, hopelessness or self-doubt which may lead to depression.

6)___**C**____ Results in back aches, neck aches, migraines, insomnia, ulcers, constant colds, allergies, and heart problems.

7)___**D**____ This type of burnout is where a person becomes disillusioned or, feels like giving up, believing that others, including God, has given up on them.

   a)Job Burn-out; b) Mental Burn-out; c) Physical Burn-out; d) Spiritual Burn-out

8)___**B**____ Difficulty concentrating or paying attention, decreased self-esteem, disenchantment, disorientation, or confusion..

9)____**A**____ Prolonged hours, resulting in personal stress.

10)___**D**____ Where people think they are the only ones who have the power to help correct their own situations.

FILL IN THE BLANKS:

11)_____*Burnout*_____ is a major reason why American industries have a hard time achieving gains in productivity.

12) Workaholics are motivated by ___*fear*___ or ___*greed*___ .

13) To you, everyone is wrong and you are the only one that is right. That is called. ___*depersonalization*___ .

14) ___*Co-dependency*___ is an inability to experience wholeness or to function adequately without the certainty that one is being actively cared for by another. In other words, being a parasite.

15) ***Passive Dependent Personality Disorder*** is a disorder whereby people are seeking to be loved, but have no energy left to love.

CIRCLE "T" FOR TRUE AND "F" FOR FALSE FOR THE FOLLOWING:

16)   **T**   F   "Depersonalization" is when you start looking down and talking down to people.

17)   **T**   F   People who experience "burnout" usually show feelings of bitterness, anger and resentment because they feel unappreciated for their efforts.

18)   T   **F**   The most tragic burnout cases tend to be people who are the least committed.

19)   **T**   F   In recovering from burnout, you must first recognize that you are burned out.

20)   *T*   F   People need to occasionally allow themselves a time to fail and forgive themselves when they do.

21)   T   *F*   Most people who are burned out are led, not driven.

22)   *T*   F   When someone says that they "can't live without you," that person is in a state of co-dependency.

23)   *T*   F   Dependent people concern themselves about what others can do for them to the exclusion of what they can do for themselves.

24)   *T*   F   Passive dependency has its root in a lack of parental love.

25)   *T*   F   Passive dependent people are endlessly angry, because they constantly feel let down by others who, in reality, can never fulfill all their needs or make them happy.

RECOVERY TEST #3 ANSWER KEY
(Answers are in bold and italics)

1) FORGIVENESS MAY BE BLOCKED BY YOUR OWN_____THAT YOU'VE BEEN HURT.

    a) anger
    b) acceptance
    c) denial

2) PRAYING FOR PEOPLE TO GET HEALED WHO REFUSE TO _____IS AN EXERCISE IN FUTILITY.

    a) move on
    b) forgive
    c) speak in tongues

3) YOUR _____ REFLECTS THE WILLINGNESS OF YOUR HEART.

    a) attitude
    b) arrogance
    c) anger

4) YOUR ANGER ALWAYS REFLECTS YOUR_____:

    a) attitude
    b) arrogance
    c) anger

5) "DON'T LET THE SUN GO DOWN WHILE YOU ARE STILL ANGRY." WHERE IS THIS SCRIPTURE FOUND?

    a) Ephesians 4:6
    b) Ephesians 4:26
    c) Ephesians 2:6

SHORT ANSWER

6) Why is the heart like a broken arm? Explain the analogy.

It needs to be immobilized, taken out of action, until it can heal.

7) How does God like to get revenge for His children?

He promotes you over your enemies.

CIRCLE "T" FOR TRUE AND "F" FOR FALSE FOR THE FOLLOWING:

8)   T   *F*   Forgiveness is just forgetting.

9)   T   *F*   Forgetting something can be done at will.

10) T   *F*   Forgiveness means that the other person was right and that you were wrong.

11) *T*   F   Forgiveness is an act of your will.

12) **T**   F   The root of forgiveness is having love.

13) T   **F**   Forgiveness means that you agree with what they did.

14) **T**   F   You are chained to the person whom you don't forgive. You are chained to that sin, offense, event, memory, etc.

15) **T**   F   Forgiveness does not mean that all the pain vanishes instantly.

16) **T**   F   Unforgiveness means that the other person is controlling you.

17) **T**   F   Forgiveness is a wound that has been treated.

18) **T**   F   It takes compassion to forgive people.

19) **T**   F   Real forgiveness comes from the heart.

20) **T**   F   Forgiving someone means that you are willing to reconcile an offense (even if the other person doesn't want to).

FILL IN THE BLANK

21) A man's going to tell you what he's____*thinking*____, but a woman is going to tell you what she's____*feeling*_____ because she's directly in touch with her emotions.

FILL IN THE BLANKS WITH THE TECHNIQUES USED TO AVOID FEELINGS

22) *Intellectualizing* means that you try to keep your thoughts and conversations on rational things when you become emotional.

23) *Minimizing* is when a person is "down-playing" a bad experience (i.e., "He hit me in the head, but at least he didn't kill me).

24) *Isolating* is when you retreat into your own private world as a form of escapism, going into a shell.

25) *Swallowing the feeling* is when you are on the verge of being upset, you sigh deeply, take deep breaths, and swallow with a gulp. You engage in physical activities that hold back feelings.

26) *Taking care of others* is when you focus on someone else's problems rather than your own problems. You're eager to help solve someone else's problems but don't want to solve your own.

FILL IN THE BLANK

27) Like a grape, pressure reveals what is on the *inside* of you.

RECOVERY TEST #4 ANSWER KEY

(Includes review questions from previous chapters. Answers are in bold and italics)

1) WHEN YOU LOVE YOURSELF TOO MUCH, YOU CAN BECOME:

   a) masochistic

   b) narcissistic

   c) pessimistic

2) WHAT ARE THE THREE TYPES OF LOVE?

   a) AGAPE

   b) PHILEO

   c) EROS

3) ___*Agape*___ means God's unconditional love.

CIRCLE "T" FOR TRUE AND "F" FOR FALSE FOR THE FOLLOWING:

4) *T*   F   If you don't love yourself enough, you will develop low self-esteem.

5) *T*   F   If you're not loving yourself, you are in sin.

6) *T*   F   I John 4:8 says, "For God is love.".

7) *T*   F   One of the many reasons why God tells us not to have any fellowship with unbelievers is because a nonbeliever doesn't have a revelation of love.

8) T   *F*   One does not need professional help or any other outside help to get through grief if he/she is saved. God is all we need.

SHORT ANSWERS:

9) Why is it important not to take on new responsibilities when you're recovering from emotional hurts?

   You could become re-wounded

10) Is it wise to enter into a relationship with a person who's been through hurt? Why or why not?

   No. You may not want to wait until that person is healed to have a healthy relationship. That person cannot address your needs.

11) Why is rekindling old relationships the biggest mistake you can make when coming out of a bad situation?

   Without receiving your healing, you may repeat your mistake.

12) Why is it important to have a good (saved) friend (of the same sex) to talk to before getting involved again?

   You need someone who can see the situation clearly and give you sound advice.

13) What does drinking water have to do with healing in your body?

   Drinking water keeps your body flushed of toxins which could build up and slow down your healing.

14) The way out of grief is going _**through it**___ .

15) What is one of life's most valuable lessons?

Letting go.

16) In letting go, you have to choose being happy over ...

Being unhappy; dwelling on negative thoughts.

17) List five things discussed in this manual to help us get through grief.

1. **Having a support group, a pastor, or counseling**

2. **Drinking adequate amounts of water**

3. **Following an adequate nutritional plan**

4. **Getting sufficient amount of rest**

5. **Getting adequate exercise within the bounds of your limitations**

CIRCLE "T" FOR TRUE AND "F" FOR FALSE FOR THE FOLLOWING:

18) **T** F When you are angry with someone, you are chained to that offense. You are chained to them in your memory.

19) T **F** It is possible to wait grief out.

20) *T* F   Negative thinking is mental malpractice.

21) T *F*   It is possible to let go (mentally) of a bad relationship even if you see yourself as a victim.

22) *T* F   Blame and guilt will distract you from your real purpose in God.

23) *T* F   Our self-image is the blueprint that tells exactly how we will behave, who we will mix with, what we will try, and what we will avoid.

24) T *F*   Our self-image does not necessarily determine how much we will accomplish in life.

25) LIST 5 OUT OF 10 <u>POOR SELF-IMAGE TRAITS</u> DISCUSSED IN THIS SECTION.

1. **Jealousy**
2. **Negative self-talk**
3. **Guilt**
4. **Failure to give compliments; non-acceptance of compliments**
5. **Not taking on your own needs**
6. **Failure to give affection**
7. **Inability to receive and enjoy affection**
8. **Criticism of others**
9. **Comparison of yourself with others**
10. **Constant poor health**

Appendix B: References

References

When compiling this book, I referred to my own life's experiences, counseling as a Pastor of a local church and as an Apostle for ministries throughout the world, as well as to my personal recovery from loss and grief.

Other references include the following:

Gary A. Collins, Ph.D., Christian Counseling: A Comprehensive Guide, revised edition (Dallas: Word Publishing, 1988).

Elisabeth Kubler-Ross, On Death and Dying (New York: Macmillan, 1969).

To request a complete catalog featuring books or video and audio tapes
by Apostle Clifford E. Turner, Ph.D.,
or to contact him for speaking engagements, please write or call:

Liberty Temple
Full Gospel Church and World Outreach Ministries
2233 West 79th Street
Chicago, Illinois 60620

(312) 737-6369
(312) 737-7124 fax